PRAISE FOR
Effective Superintendent–School Board Practices

"[This book] clearly lays out the important role the superintendent has in leading the district in partnership with the board of education. This book is loaded with practical tips and pearls of wisdom. It is an easy read with loads of good examples . . . well worth the time of every current and aspiring superintendent and school board member!"

—*Anne Bryant, Executive Director*
National School Board Association

"The authors of *Effective Superintendent–School Board Practices* have filled a gap in the literature by providing a practical, experienced-based look at how superintendents should approach the most important relationship in their professional lives. Working effectively with school boards is what it is all about and this book shows you how."

—*Paul D. Houston, Executive Director*
American Association of School Administrators

"The success of a school district is determined at least in part by the ability of the school board and superintendent to develop a constructive working relationship. This book provides practical insights and useful ideas that will prove to be helpful to district leaders who are serious about keeping the educational interest of children first among their priorities."

—*Pedro A. Noguera, Professor*
Steinhardt School of Education, New York University

"A wonderful, clear, concise, and jargon-free primer on how to be a successful superintendent. . . . Not only is this book must reading for anyone who aspires to be a superintendent, it would be a real plus for school board members. As a former school board member myself, I would have benefited from having a better understanding of the myriad challenges facing the superintendent."

—*Dede Alpert, California State Assembly Member*
Former California State Senator

"This book is a must 'read and keep' for students interested in the superintendency, as well as new and veteran superintendents. An outstanding field book for those interested in down-to-earth strategies needed to navigate the complexities of providing leadership in school districts."

—*General Davie, Jr.*
Retired Superintendent of Schools, Citrus Heights, CA

"This book is a very useful tool in building school district governance teams. The collective wisdom of the authors will provide valuable insight to superintendents and school board members, alike, as they strive to provide a high-quality education for all of the children in their districts."

—*Luan B. Rivera, President*
California State Boards Association

EFFECTIVE
SUPERINTENDENT–
SCHOOL BOARD
PRACTICES

Strategies for Developing and Maintaining Good Relationships With Your Board

Rene S. Townsend   Gloria L. Johnston   Gwen E. Gross

Peggy Lynch   Lorraine Garcy   Benita Roberts   Patricia B. Novotney

CORWIN PRESS
A SAGE Publications Company
Thousand Oaks, CA 91320

For information:

Corwin Press
A Sage Publications Company
2455 Teller Road
Thousand Oaks, California 91320
www.corwinpress.com

Sage Publications Ltd.
1 Oliver's Yard
55 City Road
London EC1Y 1SP
United Kingdom

Sage Publications India Pvt. Ltd.
B–42, Panchsheel Enclave
Post Box 4109
New Delhi 110 017 India

Printed in the United States of America

Library of Congress Cataloging-in-Publication Data

Effective superintendent–school board practices: Strategies for developing and maintaining good relationships with your board / Rene S. Townsend . . . [et al.].
    p. cm.
Includes bibliographical references and index.
ISBN 1-4129-4040-0; 978-1-4129-4040-5 (cloth) — ISBN 1-4129-4041-9; 978-1-4129-4041-2 (pbk.)
    1. School board–superintendent relationships. I. Townsend, Rene S.
LB2831.E39 2007
379.1'531—dc22

                                        2006013311

This book is printed on acid-free paper.

06   07   08   09   10   10 9 8 7 6 5 4 3 2 1

Acquisitions Editor:	Elizabeth Brenkus
Editorial Assistant:	Desirée Enayati
Production Editor:	Melanie Birdsall
Typesetter:	C&M Digitals (P) Ltd.
Copy Editor:	Taryn L. Bigelow
Indexer:	Michael Ferreira
Cover Designer:	Audrey Snodgrass

Contents

Introduction

He must not take as personal the criticisms, reverses, and even the humiliations of which he must expect and accept his full share. He must not underestimate to himself the value of his services nor must he expect the people to appreciate fully what he is doing for them.
—Ellwood P. Cubberly

In a time of increasing national and state pressure to improve public schools, exceptional leadership has never been more important. Public education is facing a shrinking pool of candidates for the superintendency and there is a groundswell of superintendents expressing their sense of isolation, concern, and even discontent with their profession. Effective board-superintendent governance teams are critical to student achievement and district progress, yet the tenure of superintendents continues to be relatively short, especially in large and urban school districts.

In spite of many years of experience spent as classroom teachers, principals, and central office administrators, few superintendents will claim they were well prepared to be a school district superintendent when they accepted their first contract. Most of them will explain that from the minute they began the job, they continued to learn something new about their role every day. In fact, an ongoing conversation among "sitting" superintendents is that the only people who really know how to be superintendents are those who no longer do it AND have the time to think and reflect on this complex job. One of the reasons for this comment is the crucial nature of working with school board members and boards as a governance team.

Aspiring superintendents observe their superintendents at work; seek out training opportunities through their professional associations, colleges, and universities; and attend school board association workshops. They read books, journal articles, and research studies about leadership and the superintendency. Others conduct interviews and even shadow current superintendents in an effort to learn about the job. Many are mentored by their own superintendents or encouraged to go to work with well-known superintendents in neighboring districts to observe a highly regarded leader firsthand.

Although aspiring superintendents typically learn many strategies and leadership skills through these opportunities, rarely do they learn how to work with school boards. In general, new superintendents find they don't quite know how to prioritize their work and ensure that board members actually become an important part of their work. It is not uncommon for new superintendents to complain that they cannot get their work done because their board members and related board meeting tasks take up too much of their time. Veteran superintendents remind them that the board IS their work, and only an effective board-superintendent governance team can move the district forward to meet district goals.

Our primary purpose in writing this book is to help superintendents and board members develop effective strategies for successful school district governance that will lead to high-performing school districts. In various communities across the country, we also encourage school board members—referred to as trustees, directors, or school committee members—who are considering running for election or appointment to a board, to make this book a "must read" as they prepare for their new role. Once they occupy their positions as board members, this book can be used further as a training manual for board-superintendent teams. Professionals who coach superintendents and boards will find this book a tool useful in building a high-performing governance team.

Educators considering application to their first superintendency or those planning a move to another school district superintendency will find lessons in this book that will guide them throughout their day-to-day work and help them avoid many opportunities for disaster in their role as leaders. It is intended to be meaningful for those who read it regardless of where they are in their careers (from beginners to veterans) and regardless of their school district location, size, or type.

We believe this book will contribute to demystifying superintendent-board relationships and will serve all readers as a practical handbook and guide to successful performance. Students who are studying institutional governance will find the authentic stories and their analyses provide valuable insights into the real world of local leadership and governance. This volume can be used by professional associations and universities, and as part of certification programs and capstone projects designed to prepare superintendents. Although it is not intended to be a research book, it does include references to a professional body of literature that informs the work of superintendents and boards.

This book is written by a team of seven experienced superintendents with demonstrated track records of success. In our combined 84 years serving as superintendents in 16 urban, rural, and suburban school districts, working with 137 board members, the seven of us learned critical lessons firsthand. We have included stories about our successes, problems, mistakes, and failures as well as many tantalizing dilemmas that are a constant ingredient in the work of the superintendency.

Frequently, superintendents and boards get in trouble before they even know it. This book is intended to help governance teams avoid trouble and maintain their focus on the core work of student achievement.

The knowledge, skills, and strategies we describe will teach and inspire current and future leaders based on the experiences of practitioners who have learned what works and what doesn't. It is written by and for practitioners who "get it." Our candid stories reveal the inside workings of board-superintendent interactions and present in-depth analysis of actions and events.

Concrete suggestions for improving practice and practical strategies provide the foundation for the reader's self-reflection. This introspection can lead to the creation of an individual professional development plan to enhance board and superintendent working relationships and provide valuable opportunities for individual and group coaching to improve performance.

Five chapters describe the experiences of superintendents and governance boards from the perspective of superintendents. Chapter 1, Building Relationships, focuses on how to begin as a superintendent and establish a strong working relationship with school board members. Chapter 2, Creating a Team, describes strategies that contribute to developing and maintaining an effective team. Chapter 3, Staying Focused, drives to the heart of the district's purpose—improving student achievement—and addresses the importance of mission, goals, and prioritizing strategies. Chapter 4 is about Managing Conflict. Regardless of our diligence in preparation, things happen that we wish didn't. People and situations are unpredictable, and we describe ways to manage them effectively. Finally, at some point in our careers, it is time to move on or think strategically about succession planning, the topic of Chapter 5. Whether a superintendent is moving on to another district or retiring, there are important considerations—both personally and for the organization as a whole and all of the individual stakeholders.

Each chapter provides a brief overview of specific concepts related to the chapter's theme as well as a set of self-assessment questions that invite the reader to consider specific learning and to think reflectively throughout the chapter. Each chapter shares real-life vignettes that describe actions and situations experienced by superintendents and district staff. These stories bring to life the concepts we discuss and reflect what a superintendent could experience on any given day. The analysis that follows each vignette highlights the problems, successes, key points, and useful practices for the reader to consider. Finally, each chapter closes with a summary that includes suggested action steps intended to improve the quality of performance and outcomes.

We had a great time serving as superintendents and a great time preparing this book for our readers. We hope you enjoy it!

Acknowledgments

These are not typical acknowledgments. We decided we needed to acknowledge one another, not just for writing this book together, but for the support and joy we have given one another during the past nine years. We came together initially as a group of practicing superintendents who believed in the importance of telling our stories to help others who are committed to improving student achievement. What happened over the next nine years was the development of a strong bond of collegiality and deep friendship.

We met at each other's homes, at conferences, and in our respective school district offices. We shared professional successes and failures, personal celebrations and tragedies, laughed and cried together, and enriched the lives of one another.

We published our first book, *Eight at the Top: A View Inside Public Education,* in 2002. We knew that was just a beginning and started planning the next project immediately. It is always a challenge to get busy people together for a weekend of planning and writing, but somehow we managed to do that several times a year. Gloria was the one who was in charge of setting the dates, making the plans, and pushing for the next work session. Gwen was the optimistic energizer in the group who would speak up first about her willingness to juggle a busy schedule and make the dates work. Peggy would ensure we had a detailed agenda prepared in advance so we would make the most of our time together. During our work sessions, Benita would share lively grounded stories that sparked more ideas, and we always counted on Pat to keep us focused on the task in front of us. It was very easy to get caught up in reminiscing about the past or planning other projects for the future. Rene's calm confidence in our ability to produce good work and Lori's amazing computer and organizational skills were the engines for our finished product. Each person's contributions made this experience of teamwork a unique and powerful experience. We are proud to have completed what we believe is a book that can be of great value to others and to have modeled for others a way for professionals to share their experiences and expertise. We congratulate

and thank one another for our perseverance and continuous belief in what-
can be accomplished by a committed group of people.

Corwin Press gratefully acknowledges the contributions of the following
individuals:

Mary Lynne Derrington
Superintendent
Blaine School District
Blaine, WA

James Halley
Superintendent
North Kingstown Public Schools
Kingstown, RI

Douglas Gordon Hesbol
Superintendent
Laraway CCSD #70-C
Joliet, IL

Kevin Hollenbeck
Trustee
Board of Education
Portage, MI

Rob Kesselring
Director
Staff Development Programs
    and Faculty Retreats
Youth Frontiers, Inc.
Minneapolis, MN

Gina Segobiano
Superintendent
Signal Hill School District #181
Belleville, IL

Glen Sewell
Principal/Superintendent
Wheatland Union High
    School District
Wheatland, CA

Caryl Thomason
Assistant Superintendent for
    Curriculum, Instruction,
    and Assessment
Cheyenne Mountain District 12
Colorado Springs, CO

Karen Tichy
Associate Superintendent
    for Instruction
Catholic Education Office
St. Louis, MO

Linda Vogel
Assistant Professor
Educational Leadership
    and Policy Studies
University of Northern Colorado
Greeley, CO

Steve Zsiray
Principal/CEO
Early College High School
College of Education
    and Human Services
Utah State University
Logan, UT

About the Authors

Rene S. Townsend is managing partner of Leadership Associates, a superintendent-executive search firm, and executive director of the Urban Education Dialog and Public School Services. Previously, Rene was a teacher, principal, deputy superintendent, and a superintendent for two California school districts.

In addition to coauthoring *Eight at the Top: A View Inside Public Education* with six of the current authors, Rene and two colleagues authored *A Practical Guide to Effective School Board Meetings*. She has also written numerous articles and book reviews. Rene chaired the California State Superintendents' Committee, the annual state superintendents symposium, and has won awards in leadership, curriculum, and peacemaking. She earned her BS from the University of Washington, master's from San Diego State, and doctorate from Northern Arizona University.

Gloria L. Johnston is dean of the School of Education at National University, headquartered in San Diego, California. She retired from PreK–12 education in 2006, after nearly 40 years of service as a teacher, principal, central office administrator, and 12 years as a superintendent. She worked in urban, suburban, and rural school districts in Illinois, California, and Caracas, Venezuela.

She received her AA degree from Elgin Community College, a BS in Humanities (magna cum laude), an MS in Bilingual/Bicultural Education from Northern Illinois University, and a PhD in Public Policy Analysis from the University of Illinois at Chicago.

Over the years, she has been a speaker at many state and national conferences, served on national educational committees, been awarded major professional development grants, and coauthored the book *Eight at the Top: A View Inside Public Education,* a collection of stories about the work of school district superintendents. She has been an active community member serving on civic and educational boards and continues to coach and mentor aspiring and practicing school administrators. She has two children and three grandchildren who live close by.

Gwen E. Gross, prior to joining the Manhattan Beach Unified School District as the superintendent of schools, served as the superintendent of Beverly Hills Unified, Ojai Unified, and Hermosa Beach City School District. In addition to her 15 years as a superintendent, she has been an elementary and middle grades teacher, principal, director of operations, and faculty member at universities in the Midwest and on the West Coast.

She was named as one of the "Top 100 Educators in North America" and was honored as the "2005 Superintendent of the Year" by Pepperdine University, where she has served as an adjunct professor of Education Leadership for 10 years.

Dr. Gross is active in many community and professional organizations and has held leadership positions in many of them, particularly with the Association of California School Administrators (ACSA), where she has chaired the New Superintendents' Annual Symposium, has been chosen to chair the 2007 superintendent symposium, serves as the vice chair of the State Superintendents' Committee, and has been named a Tri-County Superintendent of the Year.

Together with several other superintendents, Gwen coauthored *Eight at the Top: A View Inside Public Education* and she is a bimonthly columnist for the *Beach Reporter* newspaper serving Los Angeles County's South Bay area.

Dr. Gross is a graduate of University of Wisconsin (BA), University of Akron (MA), and Kent State University (PhD), and she received a Post-Doctoral Certificate from Harvard University. Her husband Jerry is a retired superintendent, and together they have three adult children.

Peggy Lynch is the superintendent of the San Dieguito Union High School District located in the northern part of San Diego County. Prior to San Dieguito, she was the superintendent in Brea Olinda Unified School District in Orange County, California. Her career spans 35 years and includes middle and high school teaching, high school assistant principal and principal, and assistant superintendent.

Peggy serves on the San Diego County Department of Education Achievement Gap Task Force, as well as other county advisory committees. She has chaired the Superintendents' Symposium Committee for the Association of California School Administrators (ACSA), as well as chairing the organization's annual conference. In Orange County, she served as chair of the County Superintendents' organization. Her memberships include Southern California Superintendents, Suburban School Superintendents, American Association of School Administrators (AASA), and ACSA.

She received her undergraduate degree from Parsons College in Iowa, her master's from California State University, Fullerton, and her doctorate from the University of La Verne. Peggy and her husband Ed have been active in the arts and live in beautiful San Clemente, California.

Lorraine Garcy recently changed careers after 34 years in education. She served for 14 years as a California superintendent. Lorraine taught grades kindergarten through high school and was a site administrator and assistant superintendent prior to becoming a superintendent.

Lorraine received her bachelor's degree in Education from the University of New York, Oswego, her master's in Education Administration from the University of California, Santa Barbara, and her doctorate in School Business Administration from the University of Southern California.

Dr. Garcy served as a member of the Association of California School Administrators' (ACSA) State Superintendents' Committee, New Superintendents' Workshop Planning Committee, Superintendents' Symposium Planning Committee, and director of the Superintendent Academy, North, for administrators aspiring to be superintendents. Lorraine also served on the California School Leadership Academy Board for six years.

In 2003, the California State Assembly recognized Dr. Garcy for her service to the students of the State of California with an Assembly Resolution.

For the last three years, Dr. Garcy has been consulting with ACSA as the coordinator of a grant from the Bill & Melinda Gates Foundation to provide training for superintendents. Currently, 400 California superintendents are involved in the training.

Benita Roberts spent the last 8 years of a 34-year career in public education as a superintendent in a medium-sized California district. Since retirement in 2001, she divides her time serving on two charitable foundation boards, part-time teaching administrative courses at California State University, San Bernardino, serving in an interim capacity as a school administrator, and working in the human resources department of her family's business. She lives in Riverside, California, with her husband of 46 years, Bob.

 **Patricia B. Novotney** is an associate professor at the University of La Verne in the department of Organizational Leadership. In addition, she serves as director of the Education Division of a consulting firm called Leading & Learning, Inc., which specializes in organizational development. Previously, she spent 36 years in public school district service. The majority of her work was in school administration, where she was a principal in three Southern California school districts and superintendent in two California school districts, where she served for 13 years. Dr. Novotney has also been an adjunct professor, teaching master's and doctoral level classes at Pepperdine University, the University of Southern California, Chapman University, and the California State University campuses at Fullerton, Long Beach, and San Bernardino.

During her time as district superintendent, Dr. Novotney served as president of the Rotary Club and held offices in several other service clubs. She was also active in the Temecula, California, Chamber of Commerce. One of her community passions was her role as president of a nonprofit organization designed to work on the elimination of child abuse. During her time as superintendent, she received awards from the Rotary, Kiwanis, and Soroptimist clubs; the Temecula Chamber of Commerce and Police Department; and the California State Parent Teacher Association.

Dr. Novotney received her BS degree from Bloomsburg State University, Pennsylvania, where in 1994, she was awarded the Distinguished Alumni Service Award. She received her MS degree in Educational Administration from Chapman University, Orange, California, and her doctoral degree in Institutional Management from Pepperdine University, Los Angeles, California.

She resides in La Quinta, California, with her husband Jerrold.

Dedication

School board members represent local governance at its most fundamental level. They frequently have children enrolled in the public schools they are elected to govern and they typically own property in the community they serve. They are often business and civic leaders, active in volunteer groups, and involved in efforts to improve the quality of their communities.

School board members spend long hours away from their families attending school and related educational events, serving on committees, reading background materials, and attending board meetings that can go well into the wee hours of the morning when controversial issues bring out large groups of people who demand to be heard. They are stopped at the grocery store, dry cleaners, restaurants, and gas stations in the community by people who have complaints and concerns, and their telephones ring at all hours of the day and night with calls from their constituents.

Unfortunately, community members rarely recognize the investment school board members make once they take office. Even though veteran board members tell those who are hoping to be elected to office that the winners will face a major commitment of time and energy, it is only after they are elected that they discover how accurate the predictions are. Many also quickly learn there is little gratitude from the community or the employees for their voluntary service. They are more likely treated to large doses of criticism and even disdain when labor disputes, layoffs, school closings, or boundary changes come before them for deliberation and decision.

In spite of the many challenges and absence of "thank you's" faced by school board members, the vast majority of them display amazing resilience and maintain a clear focus on doing what is best for all students in their schools. They work together with their fellow board members and the superintendent as a governance team knowing their performance sets an example for the entire organization and their decisions have serious consequences for the youth of the community.

Our experiences as superintendents have given us the opportunity to work with 137 board members in 16 different school districts. We take this opportunity to dedicate this book to them and the thousands of school board members across the United States who so freely and generously give so much to the future of our country.

1

Building Relationships

Building effective board relationships is a continuous process. Whether a new or a seasoned veteran, the effective superintendent knows that building a solid board relationship takes priority. The position comes with endless high-priority tasks, of which the most essential is getting to personally know the board members and their interests, goals, and passions. All districts have established communication patterns, and new superintendents would be wise to honor these practices while mutually discovering new ways of assuring good communication through discussions and agreements with board members.

School board elections often bring many new challenges for superintendents. The introduction of new board members changes the composition and culture of the governance team. Whether board members are elected or appointed, the astute superintendent carefully analyzes the constituent groups represented by each board member to expand understanding of how to further build the relationships. An election also requires political astuteness and fine-tuning of relationships between and among other elected officials in the community. Whether a parent leader or community activist, an emerging politician or a former district employee, the unique perspective of each member must be carefully understood, embraced, and managed.

Building and nurturing a board member team focused on moving the district forward effectively and efficiently must be the centerpiece of the superintendent's daily work. In so doing, achievements of the past are honored and current board members' contributions to long-term goals are validated.

Self-Assessment

- What data did you gather on the district, the board, and the community prior to accepting the position?

- What are your strengths and personal focus areas as a leader and how do you match with the needs of the district and board?

- Do you know which areas of district operations and other issues each board member finds of most interest?

- Have you spent personal time with each board member to understand the communication method preferred by each?

- What processes do you use to orient board candidates to the district and to help them understand their roles and responsibilities?

- Do you know the reasons board members are on the board, what their future aspirations are, and what they hope to accomplish during their period of board service?

THE FIRST STEP

One reason superintendent turnover is high in some districts is that school boards seldom know what or who they are looking for, other than a replacement superintendent. The all-too-common result? The wrong person for the wrong job.
—Fusarelli and Jackson, 2004, p. 56

Superintendents talk about the "match" with a board of education and a district when they accept a new position. It isn't scientific, it is often nebulous, and yet superintendents know it is critical. When it is a match, they acknowledge that they can "feel it." This "feel" evolves during the beginning steps in the communication process with a board. The first sense of how the board-superintendent relationship will work begins during the interview process. During the opening conversations, board members and candidates form first impressions and thoughts about one another. Board members assess whether the candidate meets their expectations in various areas—leadership, communication, business, instruction, personality, and style. During the interview process, the candidate also assesses how the board works with a superintendent, and gauges the dynamics among board members. When the chemistry clicks between the board and one candidate, it is a match. If it "feels" right to both parties, the superintendent is hired and the relationship grows in earnest.

Vignette

When a seven-year veteran superintendent decided to seek a new job, she interviewed in two districts. Although she was a finalist in both, she did not feel either position was right for her. Shortly thereafter, a search firm contacted her with a promising opportunity.

The superintendent did her homework on the district and found that it was an excellent district with high student achievement, stable leadership, and, most important to the candidate, a strong board of education. Believing her skills would be a match for the district, she applied.

During the first round of interviews, the superintendent felt at ease with board members. They appeared intelligent, thoughtful, and knowledgeable about education. When she left the interview, she called her husband to share her thoughts and reactions. She told him she felt she might get this job—it seemed right. Later that day, she was called back for the second interview, which also went well. This interview was more informal, with give and take between her and the board members as well as between the board members themselves. Their personalities came through and it seemed a bond was beginning to form. She became increasingly confident that this was the match she was seeking. A short time later, the search firm consultant contacted her and said that if she wanted the job the board would like her to meet with them to negotiate a contract. She did, and the relationship was under way.

During contract discussions, board members' styles emerged further. In their interactions, they displayed a warm sense of humor and camaraderie. They talked with her as a partner, not an employee, and she continued to feel at ease with the group and with the conversation. Her next opportunity to interact with the board members was when they visited her current district. After the visit, she knew she was making the right decision to go to the new district. Through each step of the application and interview processes and the site visit, the superintendent discovered the place she belonged.

Analysis

Effective use of the application and interview process allows superintendent candidates to determine whether the district is the right place for them. A good match enables superintendents to get off to a good start in their new district. Critical to this match is the relationship with the board members, and it soon becomes evident to a superintendent who watches and listens carefully. Although superintendents often generate enthusiasm for their next move, it can be disastrous if this compelling desire for a change supersedes objectivity and a measured analysis of the district under consideration. Although desiring a professional change, this super-intendent wisely stepped back after her first two interviews, where she was a finalist, knowing that the match was simply not there. Her instincts told her that another opportunity would emerge more closely aligned to her long-term career goals, and that is precisely what happened.

Action Steps

1. Do thorough homework on the district's profile, learning as much as possible about all aspects of the performance levels, programs, organizational structure, successes, challenges, and focus areas.

2. Research the board's governance history, the backgrounds of former and current board members, learning as much as possible about their personal interests, goals, and personal and professional backgrounds.

3. Remember that the interview is about a match for both the board and you. Watch, listen to questions, and observe the interaction between and among the board members.

4. Trust your instincts; if it does not feel right, continue your search until you feel a connection with the community and the board.

UNDERSTANDING EACH BOARD MEMBER'S INTERESTS AND GOALS

The board-savvy superintendent makes governance a top priority. This means that the superintendent devotes the time required to become a true expert in this complex, rapidly changing field. He or she regularly dedicates a large chunk of time—somewhere in the range of 20 to 25 percent—to working directly with the board. The board-savvy superintendent is a board capacity builder par excellence.

— Eadie and Houston, 2003, p. 56

A strong board and superintendent partnership does not develop by chance. Such a partnership is grounded in the superintendent's respect for the opinions of each individual board member and communicating with each one regarding their interests and goals for the district.

Developing a structure for ongoing communication with each board member regarding their interests and goals is critical for the individual board member and to ensure the success of the whole team. Board members campaigned for the position, they committed to serving on the board, and they began their board service with high expectations, hopes, and a sincere desire to serve their constituencies. Understanding their perspectives early in their board service provides a foundation for long-term trust between the superintendent and each board member. During board members' tenure in this important district role, they will benefit from ongoing communication, support, guidance, acknowledgment, and appreciation from the superintendent.

Vignette

During a celebratory reception for a retiring superintendent, board members saluted his contributions to the district. Each of the board members spoke of their personal relationship with the superintendent and his frequent communications with them about their personal interests and how he used these to move the district forward. One member noted the superintendent always spoke about the superintendent and board being a "team of six." Another member agreed and added that he felt individually validated by the superintendent because of his personal interactions with him. "Not once were my personal interests, goals, and dreams disregarded. I was listened to and valued. The superintendent always acknowledged and appreciated my perspectives and made them part of our district's direction. He did the same for my board colleagues."

These statements were testimony to the effectiveness of the superintendent in eliciting individual board members' interests and goals for their board service. The superintendent had a sense of responsibility to ensure that every board member was respected and reinforced for their efforts on behalf of the district. Although he spent much of this time learning about the personal interests of each board member, he continually reminded them that the role of the board is to act in the best interests of all people. His message was that the most highly respected public officials are those whose personal interests and goals are balanced with the interests of the collective whole in representing the entire community.

Analysis

Gathering data about individual board members' interests, their goals, and motivations for their work on behalf of the district's children and families is essential. Without frequent personal, focused, and relaxed conversations on these topics, the superintendent cannot fully understand each board member's motivation. The effective leader sets aside time with each board member to continually assess how they feel about their accomplishments in their board role and how their desires and actions reflect their personal and professional commitment to the district. On a day-to-day basis, as the work of the district proceeds at a relentless pace, it is imperative that the superintendent not let the frequent distractions interfere with the important superintendent and board communication link.

When transitions occur with superintendent and board member retirements, positive testimonials are often those moments when leaders reflect on relationships. When leaders acknowledge their departing colleague, what is said reflects the core accomplishments of the individuals who have led the district. It is clear that frequent, conscientious communication and acknowledgement of board members' personal goals and those of their colleagues were a fitting tribute to the retiring superintendent in the vignette.

Action Steps

1. Accept the superintendent–board member communication as fundamental work of the superintendent and place priority on frequent communication with each one.

2. Meet with each board member to learn of their personal goals and aspirations for their board service.

3. Write yourself a detailed memo called "Board Members' Interests." Refer to it often and update it frequently.

4. Establish a clear agreement with each board member regarding the communication process that works best for them and honor that process during the period of time that you work together.

5. Communicate with each board member frequently, using the model that is most effective to touch base and determine if there are any current special issues or interests for which they need information.

ADAPTING COMMUNICATION METHODS

To be successful one must be willing to learn and apply new concepts and not be afraid of change.

—Barry, 2004, p. 107

Loose systems of communication in a superintendent-board relationship do not work. A strong, clear plan of coordinated communications activities with the board is critical to a successful and dynamic relationship.

Whether the superintendent is brand new to the role or a transferring leader from another district, communication with the board is a priority.

For the experienced superintendent new to a district or a long-term superintendent in a district, it is refreshing for the governance team of board and superintendent to revisit, streamline, and continually seek ways to enhance methods of communication with the board to make the relationship even stronger. Documenting what is working and what areas of communication need focus is an important task to ensure a high level of shared knowledge.

Vignette

Consider the case of a new superintendent who comes from a district that relied heavily on written communication—a lot of it! In fact, every week, she produced a major weekly update that often looked like a novella. Although it was a lot of work, she felt comfortable writing. She liked having a hard copy of meeting agendas, district goals, budgets, and other documents. Because she used this communication style with her past board, she assumed she would implement this same type of weekly written plan in her new district.

As a veteran and highly experienced superintendent, she did her due diligence by interviewing board members to learn their current practices and the previous superintendent's communication strategies. What she found out was that this board was very much a next-generation board accustomed to e-communication of events, agendas, reports, and day-to-day communication. Despite feeling a little anxious about instituting a new approach and her own skill with technology, the superintendent forged ahead with a net-savvy communication plan.

She instituted daily e-mail messages with the subject line "Heads Up" to communicate important events, schedule changes, and school events. Each Monday, she responded to questions from board members about board agenda items via e-mail, and followed up with phone calls to board members who preferred to talk personally. She and the board president used e-mail to collaborate and finalize the board meeting agenda. Ultimately, the district moved to full digital agendas for board members and staff.

Analysis

The first step in adapting to a new professional environment is the diagnosis of the strategies, structures, and processes that work effectively within the new organization. The leader must be prepared to receive information that may suggest a different protocol from a previous communication style and may initially feel outside of the comfort zone.

As was the case with our superintendent colleague adjusting to a process required by her new board, she was both challenged and strengthened by increased technological demands.

By accommodating board members' communication preferences, the superintendent was able to cultivate a culture of effective technology-based communication in her new district. Board members appreciated her willing attitude and genuine effort to make the superintendent-board relationship more productive, positive, and efficient. Board members who communicated with parents and community and business leaders felt confident because they knew in "real time" the district's direction and what was happening in the schools because of their immediate access to pertinent information. Because the board members had daily updates, they were more aware and appreciative of their superintendent's commitment to school visitations and her regular connections with principals, teachers, and students. Ultimately, this superintendent's communication plan enhanced the level of trust between her and the board, and it brought board members closer to the students they served.

Action Steps

1. Identify the types of communication you presently use and provide this information to the board.

2. Ask all board members to define the most effective strategies to ensure solid communication about district operations.

3. Decide as a group what system of communication will work best for each person, the total board, and for you.

4. Periodically evaluate your practices and adjust where appropriate.

ANOTHER ELECTION, ANOTHER CHALLENGE

Lay board members . . . frequently come to their positions with minimal understanding of the policy role of the board or the role of the individual members of a governing board.
                                        —Spillane and Regnier, 1998, p. 209

Board elections are challenging for superintendents. Informing candidates of district focus areas prior to the election, and intensive training of the newly elected improve the person or persons' ability to succeed in the new role.

Experienced superintendents with an effectively functioning board love it when there is no election, but this is a rare occurrence. When faced with an election, contentious or otherwise, superintendents help themselves and the district by thoroughly preparing every candidate for the roles and responsibilities of being a school board member. The preparation begins before the election with comprehensive candidate training and a professional development plan for the first year of board service.

Vignette

A veteran superintendent experienced six elections in her 10-year career. Her skills in board election candidate training improved over time. Facing her first election in her second district superintendency, she used her well-developed candidate preparation program.

Each of the district's divisions—instruction, business, and human resources—prepared information on the major aspects of their operations. The superintendent compiled a board candidate notebook that included the district's strategic plan, district goals, board by-laws, board processes, and other items related to current issues.

She scheduled board candidates' workshops after the filing period ended and never later than one month before the election. She invited all board members running for reelection and a current board member who was not up for reelection to provide the additional perspectives of experienced board members.

At the candidate workshop, the superintendent and assistant superintendents reviewed the contents of the notebook; shared the vision, direction, and operations of the district; and answered prospective board members' questions. As a follow-up, the superintendent offered to meet individually with board candidates to answer questions.

Time spent with candidates pays off whether or not the person is elected to the board because of the district knowledge they have gained. For the winners, the superintendent continued training after the election. Many state school boards' associations offer training for new board members. This superintendent attended these training sessions with the newly elected members so she could answer questions and relate information to their own district. Within the first six months of the new term, the superintendent had met several times individually with new board members. Periodically, she had the division leaders join them in meetings to provide ongoing education and to answer questions. This allowed other district leaders to demonstrate their leadership and knowledge. It also gave the superintendent another way to get to know the new board members by observing their interactions with staff. Following a division meeting, a new board member commented, "Between the pre-election communication and the meetings with each division, my learning curve has been cut in half."

Analysis

Preparation of board members begins before they are elected. Carefully gathered materials and structured presentations by board and district leaders help candidates learn what is expected of them should they be elected. Through this process, board members learn the culture of the district, and they gain a sense of confidence regarding their future responsibilities. Establishing a positive, open relationship with every candidate helps those who are elected be better prepared to join the governance team. Through the training process, they develop a greater depth of knowledge, which allows them to better inform their constituency regarding district operations.

Action Steps

1. With key staff, review and determine what materials will be most beneficial in helping potential new board members learn about the district and its operations.

2. Refine the materials so they are completely up-to-date, user-friendly, and not filled with educational jargon.

3. Ensure that workshop materials include job descriptions for board members and the superintendent that help to clearly delineate the roles and responsibilities of each.

4. Plan quality time for group and individual meetings and training with candidates.

5. Never stop training and informing board members.

POLITICAL FINE-TUNING

Leadership requires, at times, the willingness to explore ideas and concepts beyond the traditional ways we have always managed; the willingness to take chances, to fail, and to go right back and try again.
—Barry, 2004, p. 64

Did you ever feel like you were behind schedule and needed to act fast to avoid getting further behind? Did you ever want to do all of the preliminary work alone and surprise your board with a fail-proof plan to get out of a mess? Did you ever feel like you made the worst political blunder?

Superintendents are proactive—they are take-charge people and eager to make things happen in a positive, expeditious manner. When issues surface, it is natural for superintendents to move forward decisively to address issues that face the district.

Vignette

A small, but rapidly growing school district faced massive issues. The new superintendent found that little long-range planning had been done. District officials had never applied for state funds to build schools; they had no developer fee arrangements, no long-term school facilities plans, and limited knowledge regarding resources available from the state.

For most of its existence, the district operated quite well because growth was minimal and only a few new students joined the district each year. Community members believed that the district would remain that way. One astute board member, however, had an opposite view. This board member started to talk about how things were going to change . . . a new freeway was going to be built through the community, the schools were going to become overcrowded, a shortage of teachers would occur, and so on. These observations were shared with the entire board, and the superintendent was directed to investigate the potential future growth and report back to the board in one month.

Being the "take-charge" person she was, the superintendent sprang into action. Among many things needing immediate attention, the superintendent decided the district had to acquire several pieces of property to build schools. After all her research, she concluded that a key person to consult prior to drafting a successful plan was the county supervisor who represented the district. Furthermore, she concluded that there were several ideal school sites, but what she did not know was whether there were "political" complications with any of these sites. She believed the supervisor would be the best person to advise her—especially because this person would have a broad perspective and represented the area of the school district.

The superintendent prepared for a meeting with the supervisor, tried to anticipate questions, and brought a map designating the sites she believed would be ideal for the school district to purchase. The meeting went well. The supervisor responded positively. In fact, he gave the superintendent a "mini" lesson in geography and politics, all of which confirmed to the superintendent that the supervisor was very familiar and knowledgeable about the district and the county. By the time the superintendent left, she had the assurance that the sites were appropriate, had contact names of developers and state facilities planning individuals, and a promise that the supervisor would attend the school board meeting when she would present the plan to the board.

(Continued)

(Continued)

> On the way back to the office, the superintendent called the board president to schedule a meeting to brief her on the meeting with the supervisor and to share preliminary details of the plan. The meeting took place two days later and that was when the superintendent's big communication error was exposed. The board president felt as if she had been hit by a lightning bolt. The superintendent had done more than make a simple mistake.
>
> The board president and superintendent met at breakfast. After the usual exchange of pleasantries, the superintendent shared details about her meeting with the supervisor. She talked enthusiastically for several minutes. When she paused for a drink of water, she noticed a look on the board president's face she had never seen before. Was it pride, shock, surprise, or amazement?
>
> "I can't believe you did such a stupid thing. Don't you know that the supervisor is running for reelection and will probably be opposed by one of our board members? Of course he was helpful, he wants to win and the problem you now have is that *your* board members will not want to use the county supervisor in any way that furthers his reelection effort."
>
> The superintendent was speechless. Her local political inexperience had created a larger challenge than finding school sites. Through a great deal of hard work and newly acquired political skills, the superintendent made a quick correction in her course of action. The superintendent met with the board member with the "political aspirations," admitted her mistake, and sought her assistance on how to backtrack with the county supervisor. Her next step was to meet with the district staff to develop a comprehensive School Facilities Master Plan.

Analysis

This unintentional blunder taught the superintendent many lessons. Early on in a new position, it is imperative to work closely with the board in defining the most compelling challenges facing the district and any related political implications. Although the superintendent's intentions were meant to be outreach efforts to the community, the first constituent group to work closely with must always be the board. Investigating, gathering, and defining issues from the board's perspective must always be the first step in a new environment. "Take-charge" leadership must be tempered by thorough investigation, good information from many sources, comprehensive procedures, and common sense. When inevitable "bad news" issues do arise, it is essential to immediately share the news with the school board and at the same time demonstrate a detailed action plan focused on addressing the problem.

Action Steps

1. Use the board as your first source for defining challenging issues facing the district.

2. Be complete in researching, gathering detailed facts, and considering related political implications.

3. Talk to each board member to elicit information about the history of the district and its community and encourage them to divulge the local subtleties of the issues facing the district.

4. Even when pressed with an urgent problem, take your time to be thorough and thoughtful and cross check your knowledge with the board president to avoid surprises.

THE HIDDEN JOB DESCRIPTION

Conflicts can be destructive not only interpersonally, but organizationally as well. Breaking the downward spiral of unresolved organizational conflicts . . . requires leadership and courage.
— Cloke and Goldsmith, 2000, p. 9

When board members hire a new superintendent, they have typically discussed with one another the detailed qualities they desire for their new leader. Members come to consensus on such things as background, education, and experience. Topics not often discussed are the "other things" that individual board members believe a superintendent should do. These elusive "other things" sometimes have the greatest impact on a superintendent's relationship with an individual board member or the whole board. In the period prior to finalizing an employment agreement, it is prudent to define these unwritten guidelines when possible.

Vignette

After nine years as a successful superintendent, a veteran accepted a position with a small city district. She met with all board members to discuss their expectations of her and what they would like to see her accomplish. After her meetings, she thought she understood what it was they wanted.

A few weeks after the superintendent's arrival, one of the board members came into her office to let the superintendent know that she

(Continued)

(Continued)

was not happy with some of the new superintendent's initial actions. The superintendent was flabbergasted. She had no idea what she had done wrong, but was eager to hear what the board member had to say.

The board member said she expected that when she walked into the superintendent's office that the superintendent would stand up and greet her formally. The superintendent was not to speak with any elected official on topics that related to the district unless a board member was with her. The board member shared that she thought it inappropriate for someone who was not an elected official, such as the superintendent, to talk to an elected official about district issues. Further, she stated that she expected the superintendent to host her lunches when they went out and to purchase her alcoholic beverages at receptions that they might attend together. The board member concluded with her concerns about the superintendent's attire, indicating that she expected the superintendent to dress more professionally.

Stunned and at a loss for words, the superintendent thanked the board member for her comments and then told her she would schedule a follow-up meeting with her. The superintendent immediately called the board president. The board president expressed concern about her colleague's comments and told the superintendent that the rest of the board did not feel this way and she would support the superintendent in whatever way she felt she needed to handle the one board member. She also explained that this had happened to the last superintendent.

After considering the situation, the superintendent decided it was time for her to set a meeting and have her "there is a difference between public servant and servant" discussion with the one board member. The superintendent talked about roles and responsibilities of a superintendent and asked the board member why she felt as she did. The board member's only comment was to reiterate her personal opinion regarding what she expected of a good superintendent.

The superintendent replied that she would treat the board member with respect in the same manner as other people who came into her office, she was responsible for meeting with many individuals, and she could not be hampered by restrictions on who she could or could not speak with. She also told the board member that it was not the superintendent's job to buy food or alcoholic beverages for her or any board member. The superintendent reminded her that she worked for the board as a whole; she was their employee, not their servant, and that only the whole board could give her direction regarding job responsibilities.

After the meeting, the board member never brought up these issues again, but the relationship between the superintendent and this one board member remained strained throughout the superintendent's tenure.

Analysis

Although this interaction borders on the incredible in a professional environment, board members often have unique perspectives on the personalized job descriptions they have for their relationship with a superintendent. Following the meeting regarding the "other things" outlined by the board member, it was important to immediately communicate with the board president regarding the needs of this board member and increased understanding and consistency in expectations from all board members. Making certain that all members understand that the superintendent works with the entire board is a guideline that needs to be revisited periodically with all board members. Although a situation similar to this scenario would likely be rare or at least not this extreme, it is imperative to make an effort to understand the unique preferences and needs of each individual and balance these needs with the entire leadership body.

Action Steps

1. Gather data regarding board members' preferred communications methods.

2. Work with the board as a whole to set acceptable working norms.

3. Develop and define with the entire board a strategy for diplomatically dealing with individual board members whose needs may differ from those of the board as a whole.

4. Establish a commitment from the board that this strategy will be immediately implemented should there evolve what the superintendent determines to be unreasonable or unacceptable expectations.

THE BOARD MEMBER WHO WANTS TO BE GOVERNOR

I try to hear things through the ears of others, and see things through their eyes.

—Barry, 2004, p. 37

School board members come to their role for many reasons. Most board members are motivated to serve because of their love of children or their commitment to their community and/or to public education. A member whose true motivation is a step to higher political office often creates different dynamics among board members, some of which are negative. Despite varying motivations, the superintendent's role is to help all members to be as effective in their roles as possible. The superintendent does this by knowing and using the strengths of each board member.

Vignette

After 15 years in a previous district, an experienced superintendent moved to a new district, where she needed to adapt to a new culture. The new board had seven strong and committed members. One was a young man of 34 who had surprised the community by being elected the year before she arrived. At the time of his election, he was new to the area and had no knowledge of the history of the conservative, traditional town.

In the previous superintendent's last year, he had dealt with an ugly issue with one of the high schools, made more difficult by media attention. It fell to the outgoing superintendent to resolve. In contrast to the other board members who were troubled by the situation and the media hype, the young board member enjoyed the publicity. He seemed to relish the attention personally, no matter what it meant for the district.

At one of the first board meetings with the new superintendent, the young board member questioned whether the previous superintendent should have shared the high school situation with the board prior to its becoming public. He also brought forward a recommendation that the board consider changing the retirement agreement with the previous superintendent, a man who had successfully led the district for 12 years. The new superintendent and the other board members were completely taken by surprise. No one was happy. They managed to get through the meeting, but it was not a pleasant experience.

A few days later, the superintendent met with this young man and told him to never surprise her or his board colleagues like that again. She explained that it was her responsibility to gather information for him as she did for every board member so he would not have to ask such sensitive and potentially volatile questions in a public forum.

As she and the staff worked with him during his continuing board tenure, she began to understand the young man's actions as an ongoing need for name recognition because his ultimate plan was to run for higher office beyond his elected role in the local community. State office—maybe even governor—was his goal, and he was willing to do almost anything to have his name out in front.

The other board members recognized this and were not very supportive. They were local people who wanted board members who were devoted only to local community service. This young board member's behavior was foreign and unwelcome. The young member was bright, personable when he wanted to be, and focused on building a coalition of supporters. The superintendent's goal was to work with the other board members to recognize this young man's strengths and not let his political ambitions get in the way of the total board working to accomplish the district goals.

Fortunately, the superintendent established a good working relationship with the young man and helped him become a better board member. She worked hard to reduce the potential for "surprises" from the young member. The positive side of his political ambition was the fact that as an active and visible board member, he attended events and spoke positively about the district. In many ways, he helped the district raise its profile throughout the area.

The superintendent learned to enjoy this young go-getter. His intelligence and wit was often combined with warmth and caring. The superintendent was able to acknowledge that the young board member was ambitious and not to assume his larger goal was a negative one for her or the district. She also assisted other members to get past his personal ambition and recognize the skills he brought to the board. It was not always easy, as he sometimes caused the district to be "out there" in the public eye. Nevertheless, her acceptance and understanding of his motivations enabled her to turn a difficult and potentially explosive situation into one that strengthened the district.

Analysis

Superintendents must discover and use the strengths each board member brings to the governance team and the district. They need to understand board members' motivations, knowledge, and skills. If one or more member is politically motivated, the superintendent needs to determine how that ambition might benefit the district.

When superintendents take time to know each member and their personal and political goals, they can coach and assist each person to become a better board member. Superintendents can also help all board members acknowledge the strengths that each other member of the governance team brings to the board's effectiveness.

Action Steps

1. Meet with each board member and learn their personal motivations for being on the board.

2. Develop a good relationship with each board member and build on it to coach each person to be a better board member.

(Continued)

(Continued)

3. Talk to each board member about the strengths of each of the other members.

4. When political motivation gets in the way of board effectiveness, work with the member involved to contribute to the team; political ambitions and board member effectiveness can be compatible.

HONORING PAST BOARD MEMBER ACCOMPLISHMENTS

Each of us can look back upon someone who made a great difference in our lives, often a teacher whose wisdom or simple acts of caring made an impression upon us at a formative time. In all likelihood, it was someone who sought no recognition for their deed, other than the joy of knowing that, by their action, another's life had been made better.
—Zadra, 1999, p. 86

There is nothing more inspirational than learning the history of our school districts and honoring past leadership. Acknowledgement of the contributions, devotion, and dedication of those individuals who have preceded present leaders is a characteristic of ethical leadership.

Whether a school district is twenty, forty, or sixty years old, each has a unique and exciting history. Pioneering and courageous board members have furthered the mission of schooling in their communities over the years. They have contributed to school district progress. The superintendent-board team should acknowledge their legacy and contributions when talking about the accomplishments of the district. It is powerful when a superintendent recognizes the historical contributions of those who have led before. Validation of the past and a sincere appreciation for those who have given years of collective leadership to bring the district to its present status sends a strong symbolic message to present employees that they too create a legacy for those to follow.

Vignette

During the dedication of a new performing arts building in a district, the previous superintendents and board members were the centerpiece of the celebration. These twenty-plus participants were highly visible with their corsages and boutonnieres. Community members greeted and thanked them as they were walked down a "red carpet" entryway on the arms of current students. There was not a dry eye in the house! Dreams for this performing arts center had been forefront in the minds of members of this community for many years. Hundreds of people contributed their expertise, their ideas, and their personal funds, but the fiscal challenges of launching such a project in a small town had been daunting. After several years of effort, however, the performing arts facility was a reality and it was opened with a lavish ceremony. The involvement of the present students in hosting and honoring the previous board members was a visible cross-generational collaboration. The superintendent made certain that the entire community acknowledged the hard work and dedication of the previous district leaders and generated spirit for what the community had accomplished together. In the process, his own credibility was strengthened.

A similarly exhilarating event occurred in another district that celebrated the reopening of a renovated auditorium that had been named in honor of a previous superintendent who had retired from the district after a stellar career. Although the auditorium had long been named after the retired superintendent, most current employees had no knowledge of the character and the contributions of this man. When the auditorium reopened, the current high school principal walked the 80-year-old superintendent down the long aisle to the podium and the entire district staff, former board members, principals, superintendents, and colleagues from throughout the state cheered as the high school band played "Hail to the Chief!" Once again, the celebration moved the audience to tears and brought the district and community together.

Analysis

There are countless opportunities for superintendents to acknowledge the contributions of past boards and past administrators. For one, superintendents can deliver speeches to describe the history of the organization and explain how present buildings, traditions, policies, and procedures are a result of those who provided the early leadership. See the Action Steps below for more ideas.

Action Steps

1. Consider sharing a "tidbit of history" during board meetings that relates to the origin of a significant district tradition.

2. Consider a "Did you know?" list of highlights sharing the accomplishments of present and past board members.

(Continued)

(Continued)

---

3. Invite previous board members to leadership and board meetings to speak about the history of the district.

4. Find opportunities to invite and honor previous board members at special events.

RELATIONSHIP BUILDING NEVER ENDS

Still I am learning . . .
—Michelangelo, quoted in Zadra, 1999, p. 114

Superintendents quickly learn that building a relationship with each board member is a critical foundation for working together with the entire board as a governance team. They learn that establishing personal relationships helps the team weather uncertain and challenging times and it helps keep everyone focused on their unity of purpose and common vision for the organization on a day-to-day basis.

Relationship building only happens with conscious effort and nurturing a commitment to honor individual contributors. It is a beneficial investment of time and energy to schedule regular face-to-face meetings with board members for the express purpose of getting to know them, their concerns, and their hopes for the future. Regular meetings also help the superintendent stay in touch with the board members' points of view on specific issues in the school district and the community.

Vignette

A veteran superintendent, who thought she was usually well-informed about her board members' positions on issues and concerns, was invited to lunch by a board member to discuss whether he would run for office for a second term. He was part of the original board that hired her and they had worked well together for the past four years. She saw him as a responsible, skillful, and thoughtful board member and was anxious for him to be reelected.

She arrived at the lunch meeting prepared with three reasons why he should run again: his continued involvement would maintain a stable board focused on improving student achievement and closing the achievement gap; he possessed strong diplomacy and negotiating skills that helped the board work through contentious issues and disagreements in a spirit of teamwork; and, even though they occasionally disagreed, she enjoyed working with him. They had the same goals and expectations for the district, and he clearly understood the distinction between the role of the superintendent and the role of board members.

When she finished her list, he was quiet for a moment and said: "Oh, that isn't what I wanted to talk about at all. What I want to know is what are your plans for the future?" He went on to explain that he didn't want to stay on the board if she was planning to leave during his second term. He did not want to go through the stress and challenge of finding a new superintendent and investing time getting to know one and starting over to get the governance team focused.

As she listened to the board member talk, she realized that he was looking at this decision from a totally different point of view from hers; it renewed her awareness of how important it is to continuously communicate with board members and not assume that you know their thoughts or positions on every issue. Relationship building never ends.

Analysis

The superintendent's ability to build strong relationships with each board member is essential to the success of the governance team, and ultimately of the district. Once a relationship is established, however, the superintendent must not assume she understands the board members' perspectives and expectations on all issues. Regular opportunities to talk with and listen to each board member are critical.

Action Steps

1. Make a conscious effort to get to know each board member individually to understand the issues and concerns of each person through regularly scheduled individual meetings.

2. Do not assume to know board members' positions on issues.

3. Provide opportunities at board retreats and social events for you and the board members to share personal anecdotes, reflections, and dreams with one another.

CHAPTER SUMMARY

Establishing a trusting and collaborative relationship between school board members and between the board and superintendent is one of the highest and most essential priorities for the superintendent of schools. To build trust within an organization, the superintendent must continually focus on coaching, training, and responding to board members' needs. Board members were chosen by their communities to establish policies for local public schools, and it is a fundamental aspect of the superintendent's job to guide these individuals through the maze of legal mandates, instructional expectations, and the myriad of policies that focus on moving the district forward in meeting the varying needs of its students and the families they represent.

This foundation of trust is built from the earliest steps when board members first consider adding board service to their final job responsibilities after many years of experience. The responsibility for their success lies in the ability of superintendents to guide and focus their board members on developing policies and procedures that provide the most exceptional environments for student learning and for hiring the most talented professionals. The depth of trust between boards and superintendents is reflected in the success of students who matriculate through their 13 years of education in our nation's schools.

To ensure that the relationships are developed and maintained through the superintendent and boards' tenure, it is important to develop effective strategies, including

- Learn every aspect about the district that you will lead prior to accepting a new position to ensure that the partnership between the board and the superintendent is a personal and professional match.
- Spend time with individual board members to learn of their personal goals and aspirations for their board service.
- Establish clear agreements with board members regarding the communication links that will be the most effective match for each member's personal style and preference.
- Welcome new members to the board and spend time providing them with detailed orientation materials and an opportunity to ask questions so they understand all aspects of the district's operation. Continue educating board members throughout their tenure.
- Assess all aspects of challenging issues facing the board and communicate with the members so they are not surprised or blindsided by any actions.
- Develop written guidelines, protocols, and norms regarding personal expectations that board members have for the superintendent so there is clarity and understanding among all parties.
- Facilitate collaborative relationships among all board members, acknowledging individual strengths and contributions to the board as a collective body.

- At every opportunity, acknowledge and recognize the past leaders of the district as a way to honor their individual contributions.
- Celebrate the board and superintendent partnership with retreats and social events that focus on building relationships that will lead to more effective work on behalf of students.

2

Creating a Team

Achieving district goals requires that the governance team work together. The superintendent and board must not only create, but also maintain, a strong governance team. Creating an effective team is a learned activity, one every board member and superintendent must commit to doing.

The first step is to define and agree to the unique roles and responsibilities of each, and then to establish a set of operating procedures, called protocols, that all agree to follow. Without these protocols in place, it is very difficult to create a team that knows where it is going and how to get there. One technique to keep board members and superintendents focused is having "planned priorities." The superintendent's days should be planned around and spent on the district priorities. Communicating the superintendent's plans and activities to the board helps the board stay on target.

Other communication strategies are vital as board members must be well informed, ask questions, and prepare themselves to be effective at board meetings. Superintendents have a responsibility to use strategies for preparing the board to make difficult decisions, to maintain civility when issues may be contentious, and to help board members remain within their roles in the governance structure. A frequently overlooked strategy for keeping boards and superintendents focused is the superintendent evaluation. A facilitated process can be effective for the whole team as a way to assess progress toward goals, thus maintaining a strong team focused on providing the best education for the students.

Self-Assessment

- What is your plan for ongoing board professional development?

- Do you analyze your weekly schedule of activities and projects to see if you are spending your time on the district's priorities and then communicate these to the board?

- How do you communicate the board's roles and actions to your community?

- Do you have a process in place for board members to ask questions about agenda items prior to the meeting and to help them know how to ask questions in the public board meetings?

- Do you have a strategy for responding to board members when they ask inappropriate questions at a public board meeting?

- Do you understand the history as well as the relevance of board policies and consider the consequences when changing them?

- Does your contract include a provision for an annual written evaluation of your performance based on your job responsibilities and agreed-to goals for the year?

BOARD-SUPERINTENDENT PROTOCOLS

We recommend the board-superintendent team work together to develop a set of protocols . . . that focuses on leadership, governance, and management.

—Townsend et al., 2005, p. 147

Defining roles and responsibilities for board members and superintendents cannot be left to chance. These tasks must be straightforward and explicit. Essential to this effort is the establishment of agreements or "protocols" that establish a set of operating procedures by which board members and the superintendent agree to handle their duties.

Protocols provide the framework for interactions between members of the team and can be used to handle difficult situations. Whether the situation is one of a board member violating a protocol, or one in which a constituent challenges board actions in a public meeting, these operational procedures can help refocus the board and superintendent.

Vignette

Two members of a search firm were hired to assist members of a board in their search for a new superintendent. The district was considered to be a place with a top staff, terrific students, and supportive parents and community. The major problem was a dysfunctional board. Not that it is unusual for boards to have difficulty working together, but this board's meetings were televised, and the meetings had become the community's entertainment as a result of board antics.

The board members openly stated that they didn't like one another; they argued and they were divided on votes. Board members sat with their backs to one another in meetings, some members periodically stormed out of meetings, and they hurled accusations at one another. The rancor ratcheted up after some members of the board led a recall effort against other colleagues.

A superintendent search process often brings a board together, but members of this board were too far apart, and frankly they seemed to enjoy the drama they created. Without an agreement to work on reducing the deep divide and reaching an accord to be civil, bringing the board a pool of top superintendent candidates would be a huge challenge. The search firm members chosen to lead the effort to select a new superintendent were honest and truthful in sharing their observations. They agreed that they would continue to lead the search process only with the understanding that an initial protocol workshop would be arranged with the new superintendent as soon as he or she was hired. The board was shocked enough to unanimously agree to a workshop on effective governance with the specific goal of establishing a set of operating protocols. Despite their skepticism, all members were committed to finding a good superintendent and they were willing to give the workshop a try. The search firm consultants agreed to facilitate with cautious optimism.

Although this session did not start particularly well, board members agreed their goal was to define five or six protocols for behavior, which all of them would support, and each member would agree to uphold. Most boards adopt many more protocols, but given where this board was, a small set would be a great step forward and a realistic number that could legitimately be implemented. The search team started with a background review of effective governance, examples of protocols used by other districts, and particular ones this board might consider. The board members knew the stakes were high and this was not going to be an exercise for show. At the conclusion, they would have a list all could sign and commit to practicing at ensuing meetings. It was a tentative, but positive, "beginning."

The meeting was tough, with a couple of blowups, followed by reminders of why they were there and their obligation as community leaders to fulfill their responsibilities as trustees and their commitment to students. The final list contained six protocols, ranging from the grand and philosophical to the mundane and easily addressed. The first protocol was "To make all decisions with the best interests of the students in mind." The last was "To never bring up the recall election in a public meeting." The first protocol reminded each person of the purpose of their position, the high calling of a board member—to serve students. The last, bringing up the recall, attended to the constant jabbing they did to one another, which dropped behavior to the lowest level of school yard bullying. Collectively, the protocols were a major step forward.

To the board's credit, the processes of protocol setting and hiring a new superintendent began an era of focusing on student needs instead of on one another. They carried through with their commitment to continuing the work with the new superintendent—again not a simple task, but they did it. Members of the board never became friends, but they became increasingly civil and focused on why they were members of a board of "trustees."

Analysis

As is true with an overwhelming majority of board members, these individuals had good hearts, but initially they were a long way from wanting to give one another credit for any accomplishments. Locked into a negative spiraling pattern of behavior, they needed to be jolted out of this pattern, as it was disruptive and distracting to the district staff and the community.

The process of developing protocols may provoke a wide range of responses. Sometimes the entire team responds magnificently to setting high standards and adhering to them. The result is clear direction and a sense of confidence in the district leadership. In some cases, there are board members who only give lip service to the process. Yet the protocols remain key as they provide the rest of the team a point of reference and a standard to "reel in" a maverick board member.

The operating procedures, while not meaning that everyone thought alike, provided structure so discussions could be about ideas, not personalities. When arguments are based on people and personalities rather than on ideas, it is a loss for the democratic process and for the students. By developing the protocols with the new superintendent, the governance team began a new culture.

Action Steps

1. When going into a new district, the superintendent's employment contract must state a commitment by the board and the superintendent to ongoing training, as well as the establishment of protocols. If the current contract does not include these provisions, the superintendent should request they be added the next time the contract is renewed.

2. Creating protocols is the first step in board-superintendent development, and the process is often most effective with a skilled facilitator. The use of a facilitator allows every board member and the superintendent to be equal participants.

3. Consider the protocols as a "Leadership Compact" that describes how the district will be governed and share it widely shared with the staff and community.

4. Ensure there is ongoing superintendent-board training. As soon as possible after a new board member is elected, schedule a training session to review and reaffirm the protocols, and have the new team sign the agreement.

5. Regularly assess the effectiveness of the board and superintendent in living up to the protocols, as it is each member of the team's responsibility to make every effort to adhere to them.

USE PLANNED PRIORITIES AS A KEY COMMUNICATION STRATEGY

You can have brilliant ideas, but if you can't get them across, your ideas won't get you anywhere.

—Lee Iacocca

Superintendents quickly learn that board members do not all have the same need for information. Some board members want to know what the superintendent does on a daily basis. Others are more interested in the bigger view of your work. There are those board members who are not interested in the details of the work, but rather the results.

Communicating openly with trust and integrity and providing equal access to information to all members is a key to the success of a superintendent. One proven strategy in a comprehensive communication plan is to let board members know the details of the superintendent's work planned for each week.

New and veteran superintendents share a weekly schedule and planned priorities for each week with board members. This strategy enhances communication and helps the board and superintendent to stay focused on priorities. By sharing planned priorities, the superintendent is saying that communication with the board is important.

Vignette

A board member phoned the superintendent one day and told her she was concerned that the item on the board agenda regarding eliminating elementary busing might draw a large crowd, because after hearing from several constituents, she realized that eliminating busing that had been provided to one neighborhood for many years might be more controversial than they had thought. This action was part of the overall budget reduction process for the coming school year. As the superintendent thanked the board member for the heads-up—which would require her to prepare for additional seating and make personal contact with community leaders prior to the meeting—the board member said, "I can't tell you how much I like it that you send me your plan for the week. I use it when I need to phone you and it helps to keep us from playing phone tag. This way I know when you are most likely to be able to take my call, and it helps me to feel like a member of the team with you."

On another occasion, a different board member called the same superintendent to ask about a meeting with a teacher that was listed on the schedule. The teacher had been very vocal in the previous board election, before the superintendent had come to the district. The board member wanted to caution the superintendent about a potential problem in talking with the teacher. This information was valuable to the superintendent in preparing for the meeting. The positive feedback from the first board member and the information from the second reinforced the use of the planned priorities.

Analysis

Having strategies to share planned priorities provides the superintendent a regular opportunity to reflect on time management during the coming week. The superintendent can also set time aside quarterly to review priorities and the calendar and determine whether she is using her time as intended. In the fast-paced job of the superintendent, it is easy to become driven by a calendar of appointments rather than the goals and objectives established with the board. Checking a calendar that indicates the planned priorities for the week against time lines, deadlines, and benchmarks, can help a superintendent stay on task and stay focused.

It is important to remind board members that the tasks listed on this document are "planned," because every day doesn't always go according to what is planned. Appointments get cancelled, crises arise, and adjustments are made to the schedule in response to unanticipated needs. It is a plan open to revision each and every day. Using the planned priorities process is an invaluable communication and planning tool for the superintendent and board because it allows for and promotes feedback and solid information sharing.

Action Steps

1. Clarify your own priorities for the week.

2. Analyze your schedule to see if you are doing activities, having meetings, and so on, to meet your priorities.

3. Send your weekly schedule for the next week to the board members on the Friday before.

BOARD COMMUNICATOR

We need to ask ourselves two essential questions: What information do we need to communicate and to whom? What is the best method of communicating with each constituency?

—Townsend et al., 2005, p. 119

The superintendent has a major responsibility for keeping the staff and community informed about board decisions. In many districts, confusion exists over the board's roles and responsibilities and the superintendent and staff's roles and responsibilities. To ensure that the staff and community understand the board's role, the superintendent should develop a strategy for communicating the board's actions after every board meeting. The goal is to help stakeholders understand that the board makes policy and fiscal decisions and the superintendent and staff make decisions about the way in which board policy and fiscal decisions are put into practice.

Superintendents need to communicate newly adopted policies that govern staff work and help the staff to recognize the board members' legal standing as elected officials, and that, as their employer, the board is the ultimate decision-making body with respect to hiring, promotion, and termination. Written communication from the superintendent to the staff allows busy site administrators and other staff to remain current and informed about the district and specific board actions, without needing to wade through other communications. Reporting on the board's recognition of students, staff, and special programs in a board communication allows the staff to see that the board cares about their special efforts, and that it recognizes them frequently.

Vignette

For 18 years, a superintendent who devoted considerable thought to the most effective ways of communicating with the staff and "community influence makers" annotated items on the twice-monthly board agenda. He believed that a clearly written and annotated board agenda distributed to PTA presidents, local newspapers, civic and service club leaders, district administrators, and union leaders served a more useful purpose than the district newsletter.

He also believed the entire district staff should be informed about board actions in a one-page communication or briefing immediately following each board meeting. He called this document, "It Happened on Monday." When a holiday fell on Monday and the board met on Tuesday, he crossed out Monday and wrote Tuesday as an attention-getting device. The masthead contained the title, the meeting date, the names of the board members, and the superintendent all in colored ink. The district mission statement was in a different box. The paper color changed each year to signal a new beginning. The first heading was "Board Actions." Consent calendar items were typically not reported; only those deemed significantly important to the district as a whole were noted. All names were highlighted, which acknowledged staff members and gave them recognition for making specific recommendations. Student and staff recognition were a major part of each board agenda, so the superintendent asked principals to remind him of special awards and honors their students or staff members received and highlighted the names and their sites. "It Happened on Monday" became a document to save.

The superintendent appointed a staff member to write and edit the board communicator. Because the superintendent stressed accurate communication, at least two other staff members proofread the copy before it received the superintendent's final approval for printing. Then, the district office staff moved into action, printing and packaging the right number of copies for every site and then delivering this one-page, two-sided document to every location not later than the end of the workday. A by-product of this rapid communication was the exhilarating feeling they experienced when the staff reflected on their performance as a team dedicated to communicating important board decisions affecting the students and staff.

Analysis

By communicating board actions and highlights from the agenda to all stakeholders, the superintendent was educating them about the roles he and the board played in leading the district. "It Happened on Monday" also was a tool for building the team of staff members who read about, prepared, and distributed it.

One of the most effective strategies a superintendent can use for communicating to the district's constituents is to develop a weekly, bimonthly, or monthly document outlining district happenings. When current information is provided routinely, there is a clear sense that data are shared openly and forthrightly with individuals who have a need to know. When a superintendent places a high priority on a systematic format, the result is confidence and trust in the board and the superintendent's communication styles.

In districts where every employee has an e-mail address, attractive e-mail attachments can produce the same positive communication. The commitment to timely and accurate communication about major board actions and the board's recognition of district students and staff remain important communication strategies.

Action Steps

1. Find ways to recognize the board's role as policymakers who represent the community served by the school district.

2. Recognize that regular, timely, and accurate communication is a major strategy for demonstrating the board's commitment to students and staff.

3. Develop uncomplicated processes for communicating the board's actions to the staff and write in a simple, jargon-free, user-friendly writing style.

MAY I ASK THAT?

> *It's as simple as this. When people don't unload their opinions and feel like they have been listened to, they won't really get on board.*
>   —Lencioni, 2002, p. 94

Superintendents expect board members to make many decisions. Thus, superintendents must provide information, prepare backup materials, and make detailed presentations so board members can make well-informed decisions. Following such presentations, many superintendents assume that if board members still need more information, they will let the superintendent know.

Board members are not always trained in how to ask questions effectively or to feel confident in their knowledge of various agenda items. For the board to make effective decisions as expected by the community, superintendents should provide training and support in questioning techniques.

Vignette

A retired superintendent was appointed for a 10-month period as an interim superintendent while the board conducted the search for a new superintendent. In conjunction with the board president, the interim superintendent prepared the material for one of the first board meetings, making certain that all the appropriate backup materials were included. Because there were many "hot" items on the agenda, she met with each of the board members prior to the board meeting to review the materials. Despite these individual meetings and extensive review of the information with each of them, she was surprised at how few questions they asked about the agenda items. She made the assumption that the board understood the materials and had the information they needed to make informed decisions.

At the board meeting as each item was presented, various board members made a few statements but asked very few specific questions. The board approved the items as presented but the interim superintendent was puzzled and somewhat uncomfortable that few clarifying questions were asked related to the recommendations. This same pattern of limited statements and questions continued in subsequent meetings.

Following a board meeting, the interim superintendent met with each board member regarding her concern about such limited give-and-take. She inquired why they never asked questions before or at the board meetings. The shocking answer was that they had each been told by the previous superintendent NOT to ask questions. A couple of the board members confessed that the former superintendent told them that if they questioned his recommendations, it was a sign they were being disloyal to him and the district. Further, they said if they did ask a question in public, they were pulled into his office after the meeting and chastised. The result was a set of board members who, because they did not ask questions either before or during public board meetings, often made uninformed decisions.

The interim superintendent knew she needed to set up some professional development. Retraining was essential if these board members were going to become leaders who would make the best

(Continued)

(Continued)

decisions. Her first step was to help the board members understand the importance of their being informed and knowledgeable about the information presented, the recommendations, and the consequences of their decisions. This meant they needed to ask questions. She told them the staff and the community looked to them to make the right decisions on behalf of the students. Therefore, it was critical that they thoroughly understood the issues before them and the consequences of their decisions.

To further this understanding, the interim superintendent asked if board members were willing to have a facilitator provide training on how to ask appropriate and informed questions. Every board member was eager to do this and agreed to hire a facilitator to assist. The facilitator discussed a variety of ways to ask questions and ways not to ask them, and provided role-playing situations for them to practice. He also had board members practice questioning one another in ways that were respectful and non-threatening.

Armed with new skills, board members began asking questions at meetings with the superintendent, before the board meeting, and at board meetings. Staff and the community started to see a board that was involved in decision making, not just sitting quietly and passively. Although they approved virtually all the items the superintendent brought forward, they did it after asking questions and having thorough discussions.

Analysis

The interim superintendent enriched this board's effectiveness by recognizing the need for quality questioning techniques. She believed that the community expected the board to make informed decisions, which can only be done by asking for information and clarifying the myriad of documents the board members receive.

Superintendents must assume the role of "coach" for board members with respect to their roles, responsibilities, and behaviors. A wise superintendent provides ongoing direction and guidance with a high priority on "ongoing staff development" for all district employees, including board members. In this way, a superintendent creates a culture that emphasizes questioning, inquiry, and problem solving. With this "inquiry approach" to leadership, the board and the superintendent demonstrate to all that asking questions and the resulting healthy debate are the district's culture, a hallmark of the organization.

Action Steps

1. Have a process in place for board members to ask questions prior to the meeting and during the meeting.

2. Assess whether board members know how to ask effective questions of the superintendent, the staff, and one another in a manner that respectfully elicits the information they need to make responsible decisions.

3. With the board, determine a process for dealing with board members who ask questions in ways that are disrespectful or not helpful in achieving the goals of the district.

PREPARING THE BOARD FOR AN UPCOMING, DIFFICULT DECISION

Develop a common vision with your colleagues. Ensure all your efforts are aligned with a common sense of purpose and clear goals for your efforts.
—Lyles, 2000, p. 17

Most board agenda items are routine. Of course, every item must be done with care and quality, yet routine items rarely require a second thought. Those items that give superintendents sleepless nights are big issues, those that significantly impact policy or practice and the lives of students, staff, parents, and/or community. When asking board members to make important decisions, the superintendent must provide plans and recommendations based on data, research, and thoughtful processes.

Superintendents need to work closely with their staff to develop quality information to assist the board. They also need to develop an effective time line and process to reach a sound decision. The planning must include ways to communicate with all stakeholders to be impacted by the decision.

Vignette

To accommodate a burgeoning student population, staff in a secondary school district began planning for a new high school. Although all district schools were highly rated and students were achieving well, several board members wanted a school that would

(Continued)

(Continued)

be different from the other comprehensive high schools. The board members knew, as did the superintendent, that some students would benefit from a smaller high school without traditional sports and extracurricular activities.

The superintendent worked with her staff to create a time line, design a planning process, create a representative committee, and draft a charge to the committee. They believed a skilled, outside facilitator would be appropriate to avoid the concern of an inside bias. The superintendent wanted specific people on the committee, such as the district's chief business official, but felt it was best to let some groups pick their own representatives. For example, she believed the two employee unions should select their own representatives. Each district school would have an administrator, teacher, classified person, and parent on the committee, and each would be selected by the school.

Along with staff, the superintendent developed a preliminary plan for communicating to staff, parents, and the community. The committee's role in this process was to determine what additional means of communication members believed would provide an accurate, consistent flow of information.

The superintendent brought these draft plans to the board at a board meeting for information and discussion. Following the board's input, the superintendent called the first meeting of the committee, and together with staff, provided an overview of the process, the time line, the goals, and the responsibilities of the committee.

The charge to the committee was to do research, make visits, bring in experts, and gather whatever data were deemed necessary. The committee would then present options so board members would have choices enabling them to make informed decisions about what the old and new facilities would look like.

The time line included dates for the board to receive updates at board meetings. When the committee's recommendations were finalized, the superintendent would schedule two meetings of the board. The first meeting would be for information and discussion, and the second for board action. The superintendent knew that providing regular updates was important. When the plan was ready, it was essential for the board and public to have time to consider, ask questions, and give input before making the decision. By the time the first of the two meetings occurred, everyone felt ready to discuss the options and consequences. At the second meeting, the best option seemed evident and the board approved it unanimously.

Analysis

By developing a plan for how to proceed, the superintendent, staff, and board set the stage for an effective decision. They involved the appropriate community members, gathered information, and communicated effectively with their constituencies.

It is important to consider the best methods of communication. Superintendents should determine whether e-mail, Web sites, and translations into other languages would reach everyone affected by the pending actions. Utilizing all communication tools will enrich the process.

School leaders know the value of data-driven decision making when it comes to student achievement. The practice should be modeled in all district processes. In this example, the superintendent and board demonstrated their commitment to quality work and accountability.

Action Steps

1. Align your process to the specific issue. In the vignette, the committee was broad based with a parent and staff members from each affected school.

2. Know applicable state laws regarding public notice of committee meetings in addition to school board meetings.

3. Make sure the charge to the committee is clear. Anger and confusion arise when committee members believe they have authority they do not have.

4. Start with the deadline of when the decision must be made and work backwards. A 12-month calendar will aid decision making so it is clear when reports related to a big issue will be available to the board for information and discussion, and when action is required.

WHEN IS A CIVILITY POLICY NECESSARY?

When people are asked to consider evidence or make decisions in a group, they come to very different conclusions than when they are asked the same questions by themselves.

—Gladwell, 2000, p. 171

Because policies and procedures develop over time, it is important to know the challenges the district faced when certain policies were developed. Before changing policies and procedures, the superintendent must be astute in researching the historical origins of policies that have become standard parts of the communication links with the community.

Although the board that developed the policy may no longer be in office, the superintendent needs to assess whether the current board still sees the need to retain certain policies. It is also essential to determine the community and staff understanding of the policy and the commitment to sustaining it.

Vignette

During a period of time when board and community relationships were at an all-time low in the district, basic civility at board meetings deteriorated. Not only were relationships between board members contentious and inappropriate, but also the public interaction with the board during meetings become increasingly hostile.

Staff members dreaded board meetings and in the days prior to the meeting, a sense of anxiety and depression set in. This resulting malaise was impacting board members as well. Nit-picking, bickering, and personal attacks surfaced between board members and began to dominate board actions. Community newspapers were lambasting the board's behavior.

Board members came to realize that their behavior needed to be reined in. The community agreed. To provide direction, stability, and confidence in leadership of the district, the board chose to develop a Civility Policy, which was widely shared and used as part of regular parent communications every year.

When a new superintendent joined the district, this policy had been in place for five years as a basic communication tool. She gathered history regarding the district, the culture, and the communication structures in the district. She spoke to parents, community members, teachers, and administrators about communications with the community. She read board policies, and made notes to investigate further the origins of certain ones that appeared unique from her perspective. The Civility Policy emerged as one that needed further explanation. She asked questions regarding its origin, the continued need for it, and the negative message it could potentially give to parents, faculty, and staff new to the system. It assumed that lack of civility would prevail in interactions and could easily be read as a negative "warning" of what would happen if any inappropriate behavior might occur.

This full understanding was imperative to understand how challenging that period of time had been for the district. The policy continues to be used as a resource, but it has been deleted as part of the standard communication package sent to parents. The new superintendent's mission and vision of the district was grounded in collaboration as well as cooperative and positive communication, and this civility policy felt contradictory to those core values.

Analysis

The superintendent was wise in her research of the community and the district policies. By understanding how and why the Civility Policy had been written, she was able to examine under what conditions it might be altered or maintained. Her outside perspective enabled the board, staff, and community to reconsider its use.

When superintendents understand why policies have developed, they are better able to communicate their intent to the district and community. Should a superintendent disagree with the intent or need for a policy, an understanding of the history will help make desired changes when appropriate. The superintendent should be prepared to offer an alternative to the policy and a rationale for such action.

Action Steps

1. When questioning policies and procedures in a school district, ask questions regarding the history of why these practices exist.

2. Review the continued need for a practice with key administrators, board members, and participants who were present when the policies were originally implemented.

3. Review the written documents with key constituent groups to gather data regarding the clarity of the language in reflecting the intended message.

4. Update the policies and procedures to reflect the intentions of the current board and administrative leadership team.

5. Remove any policies that may inadvertently reflect negatively on the district.

BOARD MEETING FOLLOW-UP

Personal excellence can be achieved by a visionary goal, thorough planning, dedicated execution, and total follow-through.
—Former President Gerald Ford,
quoted by Adrain, 1997, p. 73

Occasionally, board members make individual requests for information or ask to have an item placed on a future agenda during board meetings. Most often these are not frivolous requests, but serve as responses to issues they have heard from students, parents, and possibly staff within the district. Board members feel the need to show they listen to the electorate. Some issues are new, whereas others surface repeatedly. Good superintendents listen carefully to requests, know board members' priorities, and plan for timely follow-up. Board members must have confidence in the superintendent's ability to follow up appropriately, while, at the same time, demonstrate responsiveness to their constituents.

Vignette

Over a period of twenty years, the idea of restoring a daily sixth period to the district's middle schools resurfaced. Two decades earlier, the superintendent convinced the board the way to gain the funds necessary to balance the budget and provide salary increases for teachers was to drop a period and adopt a rotating schedule. This meant students would continue having six classes, but not every day. The teachers also bargained for a five-period teaching day, meaning the district could not add a period without incurring significantly higher costs. Two succeeding superintendents gave little attention to the matter and provided little follow-up when the issue was raised.

This changed with the election of one new board member and the appointment of a new superintendent. The board member ran on a platform of improving reading performance and listening to the community's concerns. The superintendent believed his priority was to be responsive to board members' concerns.

The new board member was determined to make a difference and for the community to know it. At board meetings and in meetings with the superintendent, she always had a small book filled with notes and questions gathered from the community. At only her third school board meeting, this new board member turned to the superintendent and asked him to bring to the board a plan to restore the middle school daily sixth period. The other board members did not raise questions, so the superintendent was unable to determine if they would support such a plan.

The superintendent listened carefully to the board member's comments and diligently recorded notes. The superintendent's attention to the request indicated to the board member that she had been heard and she knew her concerns would receive follow-up either in the weekly letter to the board or as an item on the next board meeting agenda.

The new board member followed up after the meeting to see what would be done. She was satisfied that the superintendent had a plan to respond to her request. The superintendent knew that this seemingly simple request for a follow-up report was far from simple. The staff conducted surveys, provided historical data, and included research of the time on task studies. The staff's findings appeared on the next board agenda. Following the staff presentation, the board became united, resolving to continue to move forward with plans to restore the middle school sixth period.

At the next meeting, the superintendent presented current fiscal and staffing implications of the proposed change. The personnel and business assistant superintendents outlined the challenges associated with the many adjustments in hiring, negotiations, and balancing the budget. Once the superintendent felt the board understood the ramifications of the change, he placed an action item on the board agenda recommending that the board restore the middle school sixth period. The item passed unanimously, with the new member delightedly making the motion.

Analysis

Because the superintendent listened carefully to the board member and knew this issue was of concern in the community, the request was taken seriously. He also recognized the need to have data to help in the decision making. By using data and survey information, the superintendent was able to keep the issue from becoming emotional and contentious, helping the board to reach the unanimous decision.

"Follow-through" is a leadership attribute essential for success. When board members ask for follow-up data or information related to a specific board issue, it is imperative that the information needs of each board member are acknowledged to ensure that the follow-up is on target. When clarification is needed, it is incumbent on the superintendent to get this clarification so there is no question that the information presented is adequate enough to move an issue forward to decision making. It is equally essential for the analysis and follow-up to include an assessment of the ramifications of an action on all district stakeholders.

Action Steps

1. Listen carefully to board members' comments and questions. Understand each board member's priorities and readiness for change.

2. Take the time to research the history of major organizational changes so you are ready to follow up when a board member requests that you place an item on the agenda for action.

3. Understand the ramifications of a major change on all stakeholders and the organization, and provide that information to the board before recommending a change in response to a board member's request.

WHEN BOARD MEMBERS KNOW THEIR ROLES

Neither boards nor superintendents pay sufficient attention to the need to work at developing their relationships to adjust to new demands and the fraying of the boundaries of responsibility between their two roles.
—Spillane and Regnier, 1998, p. 210

Board members have an important responsibility to their constituencies. They must be attentive but not try to solve problems on their own. How they communicate their role to the community can make or break them politically. Superintendents must work with board members in defining the often-fine line between their role and that of the superintendent. It is also important to guide them in how to address situations with staff or parents who have concerns or complaints.

To assist board members in understanding their roles, asking questions can help clarify how to handle various situations. Superintendents can help define what kinds of situations board members might face with parents. They can also discuss what to do when staff members go around the superintendent to them, help board members graciously handle these situations, and provide board members with ways to redirect the employee to the right people instead of trying to solve the problem themselves.

Vignette

In his second year in a district, the superintendent wrote an annual performance evaluation of one of the principals. The evaluation was not completely glowing because he had some concerns about the principal's performance and thought there were some areas for growth. While the principal was certainly not a candidate for demotion or firing, the superintendent felt that some aspects of the principal's work could be better. The evaluation conference included a discussion of the principal's strengths, areas for growth, and steps that could be taken to address the concerns. The principal thanked the superintendent for the feedback, something that had apparently been lacking with the previous superintendent.

The principal was popular with his students, staff, and parents. He had also become somewhat close to one board member. To the superintendent's surprise, the principal went to this board member shortly after the evaluation conference. Apparently, the principal was not satisfied with the evaluation and felt the board members should know about it. It appeared that he wanted to build a coalition with some on the board in case he needed support should there not be improvement that satisfied the superintendent.

The board member, although fairly young and inexperienced, listened carefully to the concerns. To her credit, the board member told the principal that she appreciated the input, but that the principal really needed to talk to the superintendent, assuring him that the superintendent would be open to discussing the principal's concerns. She also told the principal that she would let the superintendent know about the conversation, which is exactly what the board member did.

Although upset with the principal for sharing this with a board member and not him, the superintendent was delighted that the board member called and shared the information. The strong relationship he had built with the board members and the work done on the board-superintendent roles had paid off. When the board member in question met with the superintendent to express her concern about what the principal had done in going to a board member, the superintendent also reiterated that the board member had behaved exactly as a board member should. The superintendent talked about the importance of understanding the differences between what a board member could and should do, and why the principal needed to address the issues or questions about the evaluation with the superintendent.

Analysis

Because the superintendent had worked with the board members on understanding the roles they each played in leading the district, he was able to help the board handle sticky situations. The principal learned a valuable lesson in communication and board responsibilities.

Board members have many pressures to deal with, including how to be available and to be good listeners. It is often their desire to solve problems and address the needs of their various constituencies. As a superintendent, you must understand those pressures, but also help guide board members as they respond to the issues that confront them. By working closely with board members on the protocols of their role and yours, you can help them handle awkward situations well while still being responsive to those who come to them with concerns or issues.

Action Steps

1. Review and share board member roles as defined in various organizational materials (California School Boards Association, National School Boards Association).

(Continued)

(Continued)

> 2. Discuss roles and responsibilities with each board member and with the board as a whole. Consider role-playing potentially sensitive areas where it might be difficult for a board member to disengage from a conversation with a constituent or employee.
>
> 3. Consider establishing protocols on how the board and superintendent will interact to support each other.

A FACILITATED SUPERINTENDENT EVALUATION PROCESS

No tool is more powerful than regular, formal school board evaluation of superintendent performance in maintaining a healthy board-superintendent working relationship.

—Eadie, 2005, p. 87

Improving requires feedback—fair, honest, open feedback about performance based upon a clear definition of roles and responsibilities as well as specific goals. Some superintendents have never been evaluated. Some superintendents have no written set of responsibilities or specific performance goals for the year. Without a strong evaluation process, the superintendent and board cannot mark a clear path for the work to be accomplished. The process of evaluation also models appropriate behaviors for the entire district.

Vignette

A superintendent called a consultant to ask if she would facilitate his "annual" evaluation. He had not been evaluated in three years, and the last time he was, the session degenerated into minor hostilities between board members with hard feelings that continued to fester. The consultant suggested a meeting with the board president to talk about the evaluation form, additional documents as supportive background for the board, and the format and process for the evaluation meeting.

At the planning meeting, the superintendent, board president, and consultant set forth the evaluation meeting expectations, described the consultant's role, and outlined the "deliverables" that could be expected from the consultant. The consultant also recommended a dialogue among the board members, with the superintendent present. The dialogue would focus on the superintendent's areas of responsibility critical for district success and the specific performance goals agreed to by the board and superintendent. The result of the board's discussion would be a narrative evaluation with specific statements of progress and focus areas for the future. One board member had suggested a numeric rating scale, from perhaps 1 to 5, for each performance area, but the facilitator stressed that this type of system provided the superintendent with little real feedback or direction. The board president and superintendent agreed to go with the narrative process.

Ten days prior to the evaluation meeting, documents were sent to each board member. These included the evaluation form, a copy of the district's goals, the superintendent's specific goals, the superintendent's summary of progress, and the previously agreed-to protocols. A part of the evaluation discussion would include how the board's work helped or hindered the superintendent's effectiveness.

When the meeting opened, the consultant reviewed the task and affirmed with the participants their commitment to open, honest discussion. The consultant reviewed her responsibilities. On each area of the evaluation, the consultant encouraged them to praise what was praiseworthy, to ask questions, and to raise concerns, even if they seemed minor.

During the discussion of each area (e.g., finance, educational leadership, student learning, professional development, etc.), the consultant pushed for general consensus on a statement that would go into the evaluation. After discussing all the major areas, the board members listed 10 strengths the board wanted to highlight, and 5 areas they would like the superintendent to focus on for the coming year. The focus areas were district as well as personal and professional growth areas.

A few days after the meeting, the superintendent and board members received a draft of the evaluation from the consultant. The agreement had been for the board to meet again if there were major changes or significant differences of opinion. Through the board president, however, members indicated only minor changes. Once the draft was approved, the consultant wrote a letter of recommendation for the superintendent's file. This is good personnel practice, allowing the superintendent to have a current reference for appointment to committees or for future job searches. All board members and the superintendent signed the final evaluation.

The superintendent felt this was the best feedback he had ever received at any time in his career as an administrator, and the first

(Continued)

(Continued)

indication of a really clear direction for him as a superintendent. The board president said this was the first time she felt the board had given the superintendent a comprehensive statement of his performance and clear, consistent direction for the future. She added that the presence of the facilitator made the board behave better. Students thrive only when there is consistent leadership by all the members of the governance team—the board and superintendent.

Analysis

Superintendents must take responsibility for their evaluation process. It is the board's job to evaluate, and most often it is a part of the superintendent's contract, but the fact is, it is in the superintendent's and the district's interest to make sure it is done. Regular evaluations—written evaluations—keep the lines of communication open, prevent little things from becoming big, and provide a model of best practice. People "at the top" must demonstrate single-minded, diligent, and serious efforts to improve practice as the path to district success. One way to ensure evaluation is done well and on time is to use a facilitated process.

Evaluation is done *with* not *to* the person. It is important to establish a philosophy of evaluation as a process for learning. Evaluation is the result of looking at data and honestly discussing strengths and areas for improvement. The board should model the behavior it expects of its superintendent and all district employees, and ensure that the superintendent receives fair, honest, and meaningful feedback in a performance review.

Honest conversation between all board members and the superintendent leads to clarity about specific goals and about the superintendent's work. Through dialogue, the superintendent and other board members fill in gaps in information and improve the understanding of the entire team. Only through this unified process can the board give valid future direction to the superintendent.

Action Steps

1. If an annual, written evaluation is not in the superintendent's employment contract, it must be added.

2. Establish a regular process for the evaluation and be clear about the form that will be used, the content, and the time line.

3. The evaluations should be based on agreed-to roles and responsibilities and the measurable performance goals for the year. Throughout the year, collect

evidence of progress toward meeting the goals, and keep the board informed regarding progress and challenges. At evaluation time, provide board members a summary report on goals along with the form they will use to guide their evaluation.

4. Consider using a facilitator to improve the process and the outcome. Facilitation allows all board members and the superintendent to be part of the conversation, which is difficult to do if a board member or the superintendent guides the meeting.

BOARD SELF-EVALUATION

The annual performance evaluation is your most valuable motivational tool. The only downside is that it might require you to talk . . . more than once a year.

—Adams, 1957, p. 216

Board members often comment that their evaluation is determined every four years by the voters. Certainly reelection is the ultimate evaluation, but this is not sufficient, and in fact is somewhat of a cop-out. Accountability is today's educational watchword and, if everyone in the organization is being held accountable for performance and results, the effective board holds itself to the same high accountability standards and conducts an annual self-evaluation. A board must look critically at its own performance, and model responsibility and accountability for its actions, of a nature expected of every other adult in the district.

Vignette

A board member returned from a state board member conference with the idea, and an example, of how to evaluate the board's own performance. Reluctantly, the other board members agreed to try it. The process directed board members to respond to a series of statements, rating each on a scale of 1 to 5 with 5 being "very effective." They could also write in comments if they wished. The board directed the superintendent to average the numbers and compile the comments by all board members and then send the total report back to all the members.

A real difficulty emerged with this process. It put the superintendent in a touchy situation because one board member used the

(Continued)

(Continued)

process to attack another board member, and still another made several generally disparaging remarks about the rest of the board. The superintendent knew he should send the report to the members, but realized additional problems would occur if he did so. Already strained relationships between two members would be exacerbated. In his weekly newsletter to the board, the superintendent said he preferred to talk directly with board members about this process and perhaps suggest another approach.

Each member understood the concerns. Even those who liked being able to say what they wanted realized it would create more dissension. The next option they considered was to hold a discussion at a special workshop. The problem was that some board members did not want to take one another on in a board meeting and also did not want to give a forum, with the press present, to those who were looking to point the finger of blame. Even when the discussion is healthy and there are no ulterior motives, being frank is difficult when the local reporter is sitting in the audience waiting to pounce on any board disagreements.

An additional complication was the evaluation form itself. Because it was an evaluation document provided by the state school board association, it was generic. Most items were acceptable, but some did not seem to relate to their district, so members became more frustrated and began to see the whole exercise as a waste of time.

Shortly afterward at a professional meeting, the superintendent shared his experience with his superintendent colleagues. One superintendent suggested the process she used, which was to have board members evaluate their own individual and collective performance on the protocols they developed and agreed to govern by. She said a natural time to do this was at the same session when the board did its evaluation of the superintendent.

Her rationale was that the superintendent's evaluation is partially dependent on the board's performance and board members' willingness and ability to carry out their roles and responsibilities. Her board did its own review in closed session as part of the overall superintendent's evaluation. This allowed for open, honest discussion. This made sense to the superintendent who had raised the concern. He realized that this was a good first step for his board members to arrive at a process to evaluate their own performance. When he shared these ideas with the board members, they were pleased with the new concept.

Analysis

The board member who brought the idea back took a risk because the rest of the board was reluctant. It was, however, an important step for board development. The superintendent was very astute in recognizing the potential hazards of proceeding with what first emerged from the initial evaluation comments. He also sought advice and ideas from superintendent colleagues before proceeding.

The goal of board evaluation is to improve the functioning of each member and the overall board so the superintendent and district staff can achieve the goals set for students. Every board member has a responsibility to monitor and improve his or her own behavior and actions to ensure that the focus is on the students and not on the adults.

Action Steps

1. Talk first with the board president when considering a board self-evaluation process with a focus on accountability, willingness to self-analyze, and a desire for continuous improvement.

2. Publicly praise a board willing to look at its own performance. Inform the public that the board members believe in accountability and hold themselves accountable.

3. Utilize a process of evaluation that reflects local needs.

RECOGNIZE BOARD MEMBER ACCOMPLISHMENTS

The credit should be given to those in your organization who render the hardest work.

—Phillips, 1992, p. 107

Boards of trustees regularly recognize students, staff, and community members at board meetings for their outstanding work, accomplishments, and contributions. It is also important to acknowledge and thank individual board members and the board as a team for their many contributions. Most community members have no idea of the magnitude of the role of board members. They spend long hours reading board packets and preparing for board meetings. They give up many evenings with their families to participate in board meetings and multitudes of school events. They volunteer their time in the community as members of service clubs and charitable foundations, and they attend community events as representatives of the school district. For all of this dedication, commitment, and contribution, they deserve to be recognized.

Superintendents need to understand that board members have various styles and reasons for serving. No matter what the motivation, members are making a major commitment to the success of the district and the superintendent. Recognition communicates the superintendent's respect and appreciation for their work.

Vignette

In a small district faced with major budget challenges, the superintendent and board studied the possibility of a special local tax to retain the performing arts programs. Without such an effort, it appeared that these programs would have to be eliminated.

The challenge was that the district had never attempted such a campaign. The superintendent presented information to the board on how the campaign would need to be conducted, as well as the challenges being faced. With all of this in mind, the board decided it was worth the effort and put the tax on the ballot. Much hard work went into the campaign over several months and they were thrilled when the ballot measure passed with more than 70 percent of the vote—a resounding victory.

The superintendent wanted to ensure that the community understood the leadership role board members had played in passing the tax. He decided to make a public presentation at a board meeting. He described how the board members worked as a team to successfully raise local funds that would retain essential educational programs and services that would have been lost due to budget reductions. He also explained that they raised the money from donations to pay for the campaign, met with campaign volunteer leaders each Saturday morning to map out strategies, and did phone banking and precinct walking. They delivered and placed yard signs around the community, consulted on mailers to go to registered voters, kept detailed financial records for proper filing, held campaign rallies and a picnic, and personally recruited community volunteers for all of the activities. Each one of them took on specific responsibilities and held themselves personally accountable for ensuring that their tasks were accomplished.

The audience and staff joined with the superintendent to give the board members a standing ovation for their relentless efforts to make positive contributions to the school district. The board members blushed, but nodded graciously, knowing that even though they are usually the ones to recognize others, this was a time to recognize THEIR exemplary performance.

Analysis

Board members assume many responsibilities in living up to the trust placed in them. In events such as a tax campaign, they step beyond preparing for board meetings and attending school functions. They become cheerleaders and "worker bees" to ensure quality opportunities for all students.

Superintendents need to find ways to acknowledge the efforts of individual board members and the contributions of the board as a team. This valid recognition of their contributions will engender confidence and trust in the elected leadership of the board and encourage wider support for the district's efforts. It will also encourage greater community involvement, which will provide potential new members for board leadership in the future.

Action Steps

1. Find ways to recognize individual board members and the board as a whole at board meetings and public events.

2. Publicly thank board members for their many hours of work to prepare for and participate in board meetings.

3. Make a point to learn about the many ways in which board members are engaged in the community and make a point to share that information with others.

CHAPTER SUMMARY

All students deserve the best educational environment in which to learn and reach their full potential. The quality of students' experiences depends on strong leadership at the top from the board of trustees and the superintendent. Developing a governance team requires a commitment to ongoing training for the team, understanding about each member's roles, knowledge of policies, and the evaluation of the team's work. Ultimately, the team is successful because of open communication among the members and with all constituents.

Key Strategies

- Develop a strong set of protocols to guide the work of the governance team.
- Communicate the superintendent's schedule and priorities to the board on a weekly basis.

- Develop support for board members in asking questions respectfully.
- Have in place and use a regular process to address issues when board members stray from agreed-upon protocols.
- Assist the board in making difficult decisions by providing strong processes, quality data, and broad-based involvement of those affected by the decisions.
- Implement a process for assessing policies and, when appropriate, provide rationale for change.
- Ensure that policies are current by reading law and using staff expertise.
- Learn about each board member's priorities and listen carefully to their ideas and input.
- Assess carefully the board's and the community's readiness for change when suggesting new programs in the district.
- Define and clarify the roles of the board and the superintendent on an ongoing basis.
- Have contract language that requires an annual superintendent evaluation, and use a facilitator to conduct it.
- Develop and implement a board self-evaluation process.
- Find ways to publicly acknowledge the work of the board.

3

Staying Focused

Despite the crush of day-to-day district operations, superintendents must stay focused on the goals of the district. To do this, it is essential to have a clear set of beliefs about teaching and learning, a strong mission statement, specific goals, and a system for prioritizing strategies. This is often referred to as a strategic or long-range plan and is a living document. Keeping the strategic plan alive and meaningful requires that key stakeholders review and update it on a regular basis.

Procedures for updating board policies and an effective budget development process are additional ways superintendents can keep the district focused on its mission. Boards are responsible for setting policies; the superintendents are responsible for ensuring there is a regular process for boards to review policies. The budget is a planning tool, a decision-making tool, and should reflect the board's priorities. Consensus is also a powerful tool for building and maintaining focus with the board and other district stakeholders.

Self-Assessment

- What is your process for establishing a long-range or strategic plan?
- How do you regularly report progress on the district's strategic plan and make revisions?
- What data do you use to monitor progress on district goals?

(Continued)

(Continued)

- What is your district's definition of consensus and what is its importance for the board and for members of district committees?

- What processes are in place to adopt board policies and to ensure they are kept current?

- What is your budget development process?

- How do you ensure the budget reflects the district's priorities and board-approved goals?

KEEPING THE MISSION, PHILOSOPHY, AND PRIORITIES IN THE FOREFRONT

School districts have a single focus: teaching and learning. District goals, strategies, policies, and major activities must encourage, promote, and support excellence in teaching and learning throughout the district and in every school.

—Townsend et al., 2005, p. 3

A district mission statement, core values, and beliefs evolve from a philosophy of student learning and support. The superintendent's responsibility is to guide a process of establishing priorities that are grounded in the agreed-upon philosophy and mission. The resulting agreements from this process provide the framework, a strategic plan, for the work of all members of a school district.

Vignette

The superintendent of a newly unified school district and his new governing board agreed that a top priority was to develop mission and philosophy statements to guide the building of this new organization. First, he contacted colleague superintendents and requested copies of their mission statements. Next, he obtained samples from the National School Boards Association (NSBA) and his state school boards' and administrators' organizations. Combing through all of them, he copied those he thought best matched the district.

The superintendent decided to facilitate the initial planning process and got the entire board to agree that the mission and philosophy statements would be supported unanimously. To achieve his goal, he knew he had to be over-prepared, ready to respond, and able to give examples. Completing his preparations, he met with the board president and briefed him to get his reaction and see if there were any political issues he had overlooked. After the meeting, the superintendent distributed copies of sample mission statements so board members could review them in advance to bring their comments and ideas to the workshop.

The workshop was one full day and two hours the following morning. The superintendent began with an overview of the purpose, the agenda for the day, and then asked each board member to respond to two questions: (1) What result do you want from this workshop? and (2) What contribution will you make to achieve this result?

The board agreed to ground rules and expected outcomes and turned to the task of creating a mission statement. Every board member shared specific ideas and suggestions, with the superintendent facilitating the process by writing every idea on a chart. The process was long, at times was tedious and even contentious, but, ultimately, common themes emerged and they had a draft of the new mission statement.

Next, the group used the same process to create a statement of philosophy. The superintendent guided board members to be sure there was a direct and clear relationship between the mission statement and philosophy. The day ended with a homework assignment for each board member—to come back in the morning with five to seven priorities that each saw could evolve from the mission statement and philosophy.

The next morning started with a review of the previous day's accomplishments. Board members complimented one another on their progress and confirmed that their expectations were being met. This segued perfectly into the discussion regarding district priorities. The board members shared their priorities and talked about their rationale for each one while the superintendent listed them on the chart with the mission and philosophy.

Once every idea was on the chart, the group looked for patterns, themes, and commonalities. Following further discussion and clarification, the board reached consensus on eight district priorities. The workshop ended with the board directing the superintendent to develop a communication plan to "make the district mission statement, philosophy, and priorities a living document for staff and community." The final step was scheduling a date for board members to take official action to approve their work that would guide the district.

Analysis

The daily challenges of the board-superintendent relationship must be grounded in the establishment of core values, mission, and vision statements. This superintendent's actions were effective in planning and execution. First of all, he turned to others for guidance and samples, choosing those that fit with what he knew about the district and the board members. Then, he thought through the process and decided in this instance to facilitate the workshop himself rather than use an outside facilitator. The process is important, but the commitment of the board to the process is even more critical.

The superintendent also took each piece of the process and worked it through to board consensus before moving to the next step. Building success upon success creates confidence as well as commitment. The workshop ended with specific next steps, ensuring that what the team did was not just an interesting exercise, but living documents to guide the work of this new district.

Action Steps

1. If you, as superintendent, are going to guide the process, gather information, and talk with trusted colleagues who can provide materials and insight.

2. Work directly with your board to establish a process for developing or revising your mission statement and philosophy.

3. Plan every detail and every step of the process prior to implementation.

4. Consider whether it would be most effective to facilitate the process yourself or have an outside facilitator.

TAKING THE PLAN TO OTHERS

Enlist others in a common vision by appealing to their values, interests, hopes, and dreams.
—Kouzes and Posner, 1997, p. 148

Board consensus and full superintendent support are essential. Yet a strategic plan can languish on shelves, or taken askew if other stakeholders are not involved. Board members represent the community but cannot dictate to them; their involvement is vital. Staff will bring the strategic plan to life, so their active support from throughout the district is critical.

Vignette

After her board developed a mission, philosophy, and priorities, the superintendent was charged with taking the work to staff, parents, and community. The board planned to discuss these important documents at a board meeting, but wanted to get reactions of these key stakeholders first.

To do this, the superintendent prepared a communication plan that she could use with the public, the staff, and ultimately the board. Part of the plan was a visual document, a chart showing the inter-relationships between the components and the logical flow from the mission to the philosophy to the priorities. The chart had the new mission statement and philosophy at the top, and, using a diamond-like design, the eight district priorities below. The overall effect was a representation of the connection of the internal and external communication procedures.

She distributed the document to the staff, students, parents, business and community groups, and service clubs, as well as the board, inviting their comments and suggestions. Meeting with groups, she talked about the process as well as the content. Then she just listened and took notes. There also was a system for providing written feedback that, with her listening notes, she compiled and shared with the board.

At the board meeting, the superintendent presented the original plan and key suggestions based on the feedback she received. The board was pleased with the response from staff and the public, made a few modifications, and adopted the mission, philosophy, and priorities.

The superintendent was prepared with "next steps" recommendations for the board to consider at its next meeting. One was to design a district logo pin in the shape of a diamond to reflect the eight priorities. Another was to put this logo on posters that would be displayed in each district and school office. Finally, she recommended the governing board schedule mid- and end-of-year workshops to monitor district progress and begin to consider priorities for the next year.

In addition, she told the board that the staff would develop their individual objectives according to these priorities. The progress on these objectives would be part of the report of progress to the board and serve to help the board consider priorities for the following year.

The plan and the presentation were well received and adopted unanimously at the board meeting. It was clear that board members were excited about the direction they had initiated for the district and saw the benefits of their collective efforts.

Analysis

The process of taking the board's draft of a mission, philosophy, and strategies out for reaction from other stakeholders is essential. The superintendent did more than just send out a document. She put the proposals into a visual representation showing the interrelationship of each piece.

Not only did she solicit written feedback, she personally went to the schools, the parents, and the business and community groups. The idea was not just to tell and describe but also to listen and consider, and then share what she had learned with the board. The entire process built support for an outcome that would create pride as well as focus for the years ahead.

Action Steps

1. Have a specific plan for taking the board's work to the staff and public for input.

2. Actively seek input in addition to providing opportunities for written feedback.

3. Compile the input and share it with the board so it can be used to refine the board's final product.

4. Have "next steps" recommendations to make the mission, philosophy, and goals come alive and drive the work of the staff.

UPDATING YOUR STRATEGIC PLAN

Still the question recurs "can we do better?" The dogmas of the quiet past are inadequate to the stormy present. The occasion is piled high with difficulty, and we must rise with the occasion. As our case is new, so we must think anew, and act anew.

—Former President Abraham Lincoln, quoted in Phillips, 1992, p. 137

Strategic planning is often cited as the CEO's single most effective method of moving an organization forward. In a public school district with an elected board of education, the superintendent is charged with carrying out this function and ensuring that the organization remains on the course set by the board-approved strategic plan. This is often a challenge. Each individual who serves on a board has his or her own set of expectations and priorities, and although boards typically support the strategic plan in concept, the superintendent must be vigilant to determine if the organization's focus is on course or drifting.

Regularly updating the strategic plan keeps the organization focused on major priorities. An effective process provides a way for the board, staff, and community to take an objective look at how the organization is progressing toward meeting the approved goals and objectives in the strategic plan and make course corrections where necessary. An update also reminds the board of the importance of allocating scarce resources to priorities.

Vignette

Three years after the board adopted its first five-year strategic plan, the superintendent believed the time was right to revisit the plan with the major stakeholder groups who were involved in the initial development. Some of the original participants were no longer in the district, including two of the former board members.

At a board meeting, the superintendent presented her rationale for updating the strategic plan and proposed that the full board participate with the stakeholder groups. Shortly after all board members agreed, one of the new board members told the superintendent privately that although he hated this type of meeting, he would participate. Another new member related that she was nervous about working with the administrative team because they used educational jargon she did not understand. The superintendent attempted to calm their fears by telling them that most of the work would take place in small groups, that she would make sure people used normal language, and that group leaders would be responsible for reporting out during the meeting.

The superintendent selected experienced principals from each level to serve as facilitators. All three worked with the superintendent and the coordinator of research and evaluation to design the session and develop a data book for each participant. The superintendent sent letters to the entire administrative team, representatives of each union, the chairpersons of district-level advisory committees, and the PTA council officers, outlining the session goals and their charge as participants.

The day began with a breakfast and social time for all participants, and then the board president opened the meeting thanking everyone for committing their time for this important task. The coordinator of research and evaluation reviewed the data in the participants' data books and answered questions regarding the technical aspects of the information. The superintendent responded to all other questions.

(Continued)

(Continued)

> The group agreed that the vision and mission statements continued to be on target and did not need revisiting. Next, participants worked in groups giving their perceptions of how the district was faring in meeting its goals and objectives. They talked about "threats" and barriers to success in the strategic planning process and offered "strengths" that were examples of how individual schools were working toward meeting the district's goals. Completing the morning session, the facilitators then worked with the groups to confirm each element in the plan and to ask group members to suggest any revisions to the plan's goals, objectives, and strategies.
>
> After lunch, the superintendent said the next step would be to synthesize the day's work and come to agreement on any proposed revisions. The groups reconvened for a final review and suggested only minor revisions to a few of the objectives, leaving the goals unchanged.
>
> The next day, one facilitator worked with the superintendent to prepare the report for board approval. At the next board meeting, the board complimented the staff and community participants and accepted the revisions without comment other than gratitude. Each participant received a copy of the completed report and other copies were sent to each school, department, and stakeholder group.

Analysis

Strategic planning is critical for a unified focus for everyone in the district. Just as critical is stopping periodically to ask questions: How are we doing? Are we on track? What do we need to do to improve? If we have accomplished a goal, what's next? Just as the board approved the original strategic plan, it must approve the updated plan.

A review of the strategic planning process provides the board, the superintendent, the districts' employees, and the community a continuing and dynamic opportunity to recommit to a unified effort on behalf of students.

Action Steps

1. The original strategic plan must include the provision for regular updates.

2. Set a specific date, time, and location for the revision and invite the participants in advance.

3. Give an update of progress on the original plan and clear goals for the revision process.

4. Take the revisions to the board for formal approval.

MONITORING PROGRESS OF DISTRICT GOAL ATTAINMENT

Okay, so what does it mean to act like a caring stakeholder? For us, it means protecting our stakes—being active participants in what's going on rather than passive (or apathetic) observers. It's about celebrating what's right, fixing what's wrong, and doing our part to make things better.

—Harvey and Lucia, 1998, p. 29

A major function of school board members is to monitor the progress of the district in attaining goals adopted by the board. It is easy for superintendents to let this important task take a backseat to the everyday pressures of carrying out the work in a school district. Everyone in the school community, however, is entitled to see evidence that the board and superintendent believe in regular monitoring—to receive documents and hear from staff their report on progress, or lack of progress. They also should know the plans for further improvement and additional progress toward meeting district goals. Just as classroom teachers and principals are asked to do regular monitoring and attend to meeting student achievement targets and goals at their schools, the board and superintendent need to model the same behavior.

Vignette

Until his retirement, a highly regarded veteran superintendent mentored many new superintendents. As a result of his guidance, a new superintendent scheduled three special meetings for the year to give the board members specific updates about their adopted goals. She also scheduled parts of two of these meetings as closed, or executive, sessions to focus on some aspect of her evaluation. She believed these meetings would ensure that district goals were monitored and that she would receive feedback on her performance.

(Continued)

(Continued)

> For the evaluation portion of the meeting, the board agreed with the superintendent to hire a facilitator. This would allow the superintendent to be part of the discussion. The board president also could participate and focus on the discussion rather than having to run the meeting.
>
> The superintendent worked closely with the board president and one other board member to plan and implement the special meetings at an off-campus location. The different location would signal that these meetings would not be regular business meetings. A local business agreed to host one in its conference room; a local restaurant offered to host another meeting in a special banquet room.
>
> The veteran superintendent reminded this new superintendent to distribute public notices widely to ensure attendance by local media, school district leaders, and diverse members of the community. The public had to know that the first part of the meeting would be open to them so they could see and hear presentations of the data regarding goal accomplishments. It would allow the public to observe board members engaged in dialogue, offering observations and asking questions to ensure the board members fully understood the data and information they needed to make decisions.
>
> At the first meeting, the staff shared the data, and the board engaged in healthy discussion, including some exciting ideas for the future. They then moved to executive session where, in confidence, the facilitator guided the board members and superintendent in a discussion of her performance. The setting allowed for open communication and feedback that ensured board members' concerns were addressed. The facilitator forced the board to reach consensus on a change in the specific direction of one of the superintendent's goals. After the meeting, the facilitator provided the board and superintendent with a written follow-up.

Analysis

The only way to ensure that boards monitor progress is for superintendents to schedule meetings to provide updates throughout the school year. Although data can be shared at regularly scheduled board meetings, special sessions bring notice to the board's focus on district progress toward goals. Combining these reports with a mid-year look at the superintendent's performance maintains the connection to teaching and learning.

Consider having a facilitator for the closed session. A facilitator allows every member of the board and the superintendent to participate. This means none of them are responsible for running the meeting, or bringing individuals back on track, or reducing tense feelings. The open meetings are prime opportunities for board members, superintendent, and the community to engage in important discussions using data to reinforce the district discussion and making midcourse corrections. This allows the full board and the superintendent to engage in a dialogue about the district, about the superintendent's performance, and about the future of the district.

Action Steps

1. Schedule progress report meetings regarding goal attainment several times each year.

2. Consider combining these reports with a mid-year and annual superintendent's performance evaluation.

3. Involve one or two board members in planning the agenda and presentation documents.

4. Use the data to make midcourse corrections, when necessary.

5. Use a facilitator to guide the superintendent evaluation meeting, keep everyone on track, and ensure that all members of the team participate and are heard.

WORKING FOR BOARD CONSENSUS

The power of collaboration comes from inclusion, not exclusion. . . . It's so fundamental to collaboration that I've made it the basis of the first principle: Involve the relevant stakeholders.
                                            —Strauss, 2002, p. 39

Every board has times when members disagree on critical decisions. Even board members who have spent many years working together do not expect they will always arrive at consensus. It is particularly important during these times, often highly emotional and tense ones, that the superintendent work with board members as a "governance team" with the goal of reaching consensus.

To help board members retain their own dignity and their respect for one another, superintendents have to be alert and at their best. The best way is to continue focusing the board members on the primary goals of the district, those of teaching and learning and student success. Superintendents cannot take sides and must be on guard to keep board members from having unresolved issues and conflicts with one another. Effective leaders help each member of the governance team remember that once a decision is made and regardless of their own vote, the "team" must continue working together and model a positive school district culture for the benefit of students.

Vignette

Facing a budget reduction of nearly 10 percent caused an effective board governance team to be in danger of falling apart. All members faced intense lobbying by union group leaders, staff members, parents, and community members. The conflict and stress among the board members grew.

Board members started sending one another and the superintendent terse e-mail messages that conveyed their intense emotions. Board meetings were packed with advocates and special interest groups pleading to save music, counselors, small class sizes, athletics, and more. The meetings got longer, louder, angrier, sadder, and more tearful. Some board members reacted the same way as audience members and with the same high level of emotion.

During a meeting several weeks before the final public hearing regarding proposed budget cuts, the superintendent asked the board members to commit to taking on two additional challenges. One was to find a way for the board to reach consensus while maintaining their respect for one another and accepting their diverse points of view. She pointed out that this was a team that had worked diligently to keep the focus of the district on improving student achievement, and under stress, their resolve had begun to dissipate. As a result, they were not listening to one another and communication was breaking down.

The second challenge she presented board members was for them to determine a way to communicate a single response from the board that would keep the special interest groups in the community from attacking one another and destroying the spirit of community collaboration. They agreed they would begin to work toward consensus and to commit to unified communication.

A critical first task was to agree what "consensus" meant. All board members agreed consensus would mean that they understood the decision as well as the individual elements on the basis of which the decision was made. Every member also would have an opportunity to voice his or her opinions and points of view. Finally, even if they did not totally agree with the decision, all would accept and support it.

Consensus did not mean that everyone would be happy. They would not be voting on individual elements and ideas, nor would they engage in "horse trading." The board started consensus building by establishing a subcommittee process in which two board members met with the superintendent and fiscal staff members and then brought forward a set of recommended budget reductions. The subcommittee would consider the comments and suggestions board members had made at the public hearings and to one another. They vowed they would weigh the impact of the reductions on the core business of teaching and learning and the various programs or services that had been mentioned by their colleagues as too important to cut.

After several long and tedious meetings, the board subcommittee agreed on recommendations for the final meeting that would be the blueprint for making budget reductions. They rehearsed asking questions and responding to the concerns of one another and those they expected from their fellow board members. They revised the format for presentation several times until it was easy for all to understand the recommendations.

The subcommittee's board presentation was met with surprise and pleasure as it had captured the concerns of the other three board members. The budget was adopted unanimously, which squelched the quarreling and divisiveness among unions and community groups. Not everyone was happy, but they agreed the decisions were the best that could be made given the circumstances.

Analysis

In this case, the commitment to arrive at consensus helped everyone to accept the final decision. The best time to work on consensus building, however, is before a crisis exists. A workshop or special board meeting to define and discuss processes involved in building consensus is essential, making sure that each board member understands and can support the outcomes.

Having a subcommittee study and present accurate, detailed, and documented data to the board as a whole can be a useful approach when individuals respect one another and are willing to listen to one another. A critical aspect is for the subcommittee members to be sure to hear the voices of all stakeholders. The process helps boards make difficult decisions and results in a unified front for moving the district forward in pursuit of its goals.

Action Steps

1. Get board members' agreement about the definition of consensus and the value of consensus during challenging, emotional times.
2. Keep the subcommittee and the entire board focused on the goal of arriving at consensus.
3. Reassure all of the board members that their voices will be heard.

(Continued)

(Continued)

4. Schedule carefully planned, structured subcommittee meetings with staff to ensure that all of the needed information is available for the board members.

5. Make sure that all of the detailed program information and cost details are in print to be shared at the meeting; answer questions on the spot, leaving no confusion or doubt.

MAINTAINING BOARD POLICIES

Shaping up board policies is an onerous, even Herculean, task. Yet it is a job a superintendent can use to move a district forward to a higher level of professionalism.

—Johnston et al., 2002, p. 49

Carefully crafted board policies are not simply bureaucratic encumbrances to action. Board policies incorporate the standards and rules for conducting the district's business, and as such, allow stakeholders a sense of predictability and consistency that supports the effective and efficient operation of the school district. The adoption of board policies holds board members accountable and allows them to speak with one voice as they operate as a consensus body rather than as individual legislators.

Changing local, state and federal laws, needs, and conditions require a local board to adopt policies on a regular basis. Board policies written in response to new legislation should consider local needs and local capabilities. Processes for regular review of board policies should be in place, with the superintendent ensuring that the board and cabinet members know the schedule for review. This review also allows the superintendent to remind board members of frequently referenced policies and their effects, and those that will come forward for revision.

Vignette

In her first year as superintendent in the district, the superintendent frequently was in a quandary due to the lack of written policies, out-of-date policies, or those with vague wording and/or poorly written administrative regulations. It had been the practice to recommend new policies only in response to new legislation. Clearly, it was time to act.

With the district staff, the superintendent devised a plan to review and adopt the model policies offered by the state's school boards' association. The schedule set a time line for review of each section of the policies and gave district staff a specific time frame for evaluation and recommendations for revision. Each policy would state education code and applicable laws and regulations.

The process was placed on the board agenda for approval, winning praise from board members. They knew they were behind in their policy responsibilities, but had been unsure how to proceed. Because most of the "out-of-date sections" of the district's policies dealt with operations of the board of education, the superintendent began with this section.

In her weekly letter to the board, the superintendent sent proposed changes to a few of the policies for general information, reminded the board of the time line for each section of the policy book, and asked for feedback. Despite continued requests for feedback for two months, board members did not respond. Finally, the superintendent began calling board members to ask why there was no response.

The first one she called said, "I've reviewed the policies you sent us and it feels like someone is trying to box us in." This board member frequently voiced her contempt for structure of any kind. The superintendent reminded her that the staff based the new/revised policies on the model policies of the state association of the board members and this seemed to calm her. After a few more weeks of informal review, the superintendent placed the policies on the board agenda for a "first informational reading," which would give the board time to comment publicly and make changes before the policy came back for approval.

At the meeting, the concerned board member asked that on the next agenda, the staff highlight the changes on each policy and include both the old and new policies in the board packet. The board concurred, and the superintendent placed the policies on the next agenda for a second "first reading." The board discussed a few of the policies, which were then brought back at a third meeting for approval. The board passed the policies unanimously.

Analysis

Board policies serve as an important framework for how the district will operate. For effective operation, a district needs a regular and ongoing process for reviewing and updating policies. The superintendent possesses the major responsibility for keeping them current and relevant to the district while keeping in mind that effective board policies require knowledge of local conditions and the input of various stakeholders.

This superintendent would have been well served to take time up front with board members to solicit their input on the process. Board members have different styles, so it is helpful to clarify how they wish to receive information about policy changes/revisions. Take the time to adjust the process appropriately and ensure that board members fully understand the process.

Setting policies is a major responsibility of boards and requires careful thought. To ensure sound adoption, the practice of informal review and then formal review is effective. For all but the simplest policies, consider the power of having a first informational reading at one meeting before a second and adoption reading.

Action Steps

1. Solicit concerns of board members and clarify how they wish to receive information about policy changes/revisions.

2. Keep the policy review and schedule in perspective and adjust it to ensure that board members fully understand the process.

3. Know when the absence of policy is likely to cause dysfunction in the organization.

4. Recognize that effective board policies require knowledge of local conditions and the input of various stakeholders.

5. Keep the policy-making role of the board as a major theme in district communications.

BUDGET AS A DECISION-MAKING TOOL

Budget, budgeting, or fiscal management should be thought of as providing the means to get done what you are striving for educationally. Whatever your educational program goals . . . or just holding the line on what you've got—budgeting will get you there.
                    —Spillane and Regnier, 1998, p. 101

A solid foundation of fiscal stability is essential to achieve our core mission of providing students an instructional program that will lead to success in life. One critical role a superintendent must assume is responsibility for clear and open communication regarding the district's budget. Budgets are complex, confusing, and constant objects of scrutiny. A dedicated and sharp focus on this process reaps enormous benefit and establishes credibility for the superintendent and the board. The superintendent must know the budget process and use this knowledge to adeptly explain the budget. This task cannot be delegated to the business department or the board of education. The superintendent of schools must be "front and center" in this process.

Vignette

When his district faced budget challenges that required making significant cuts, the superintendent knew he needed a clear plan for addressing issues. He knew it was critical to develop two key sets of data. First, he and the board had to agree on the creation of a budget development calendar that described every required action with an associated time line. He knew this calendar of "what's to come" was essential to reduce the inevitable anxiety related to decision making and to meet state deadlines. With a stated chronology of benchmark dates requiring board action, board members were clear about the scope of their responsibility in this process.

The superintendent also recognized that essential to the yearly budget development process was the adoption of a set of guidelines for decision making. He had his district staff develop and present a template of proposed budget guidelines for the board to review. All board members had ample opportunity to understand the details inherent in the process. After providing their input and giving direction to the superintendent, board members endorsed the guidelines, and these were shared widely throughout the district and community. By communicating the process and time line, the superintendent and board provided a transparent plan so all the stakeholders could understand and know when and how they could participate. The district's guidelines included these statements:

- Input on recommendations for cost savings and revenue enhancement will be sought by communicating with parents, faculty, staff, and board.
- Salary and benefits levels will continue to attract and retain qualified people.
- When the board authorizes a new goal, project, or program, it shall specify the allocation or reallocation of required resources.
- Budgeted expenditures shall not exceed income.

During the process of setting budget guidelines and calendar development, the superintendent advertised the meetings widely so every constituent group had an opportunity to learn about the

(Continued)

(Continued)

> budget process and provide input. This broad publication of process and calendar assured the community that the board was dedicated to a comprehensive decision-making process.
>
> This superintendent also posted the request for input, entitled "Request for Staff, Student, Parent, and Community Input," on the district's Web site. This offered another opportunity for individuals to recommend ideas to reduce expenses, raise revenues, and state rationales for their recommendations. When the superintendent's assistant posted these ideas verbatim on the Web site, it provided further evidence of the openness of the board and superintendent, while acknowledging the value of constituent "voices" in the budget development process.

Analysis

When asked, "How is the district's budget developed?" the superintendent should be able to state it and have a readily available written process for budget decision making, one that explains the process in simple, layman's language. Having a yearlong calendar, complete with specific dates and user-friendly documents, demystifies budgeting. The benefit is a more knowledgeable community, and one that trusts those in charge.

The superintendent is the district's key communicator of the budget. The superintendent is responsible for providing a set of guidelines for budget decision making that the board approves. The superintendent cannot be passive, but rather must ensure the guidelines are distributed widely and then must actively solicit input from staff and the broader community, both informally and through structured meetings. Documenting all solicited input and providing this information to the board is critical so all members of the community see their ideas are truly valued.

Action Steps

1. As the superintendent, assume responsibility as the district's key communicator of the budget.

2. Prepare, in concert with the board, a "Budget Development Calendar" that outlines every key date in the process for the year.

3. Ensure that the board approves guidelines for budget decision making.

4. Schedule structured opportunities for constituent input and publish the dates throughout the community.

5. Document all solicited input and provide this information to the community.

CHAPTER SUMMARY

For a district to meet its goals, staying focused is essential. Adults must focus on what is important in the short term and long run, always planning, implementing, analyzing, and revising programs to meet students' needs. A periodic review of the mission and philosophy is important, again staying true to a path of focusing on students and their achievement. Goals change over time to meet needs, but they must always be in alignment with the mission.

Superintendents are the key to a district staying the course by employing strategies that help governing board members do their work at the policy and goal-setting level.

Key Strategies

- Guide board members with a process through which they can establish a clear set of beliefs about teaching and learning, a strong mission statement, specific goals, and a system for prioritizing strategies—a strategic plan.
- Involve members of the staff and community in meaningful ways, seeking their input, feedback, and support.
- Keep the strategic plan alive by reviewing and updating it on a regular basis and by involving the board and key stakeholders in the community and district.
- Schedule meetings for the express purpose of discussing student progress on goal attainment.
- Build in dates for regular review of the superintendent's performance, using a facilitator when appropriate to assist all parties in actively participating in the dialogue with the superintendent.
- Use every opportunity to use data to monitor progress and make course corrections.
- Create commitment to a definition of consensus with the board and use it whenever possible.
- While preparing for budget cutting, it is important to make sure goals, processes, and time lines are outlined and understood, and that data and reports are presented in detail for the board's decision making.
- Spend time with board members to define their priorities for approaching budget decisions so there are standards against which to consider cuts or additions.
- Get and use community and staff input on budget options.
- Be the key budget communicator for the district. This is not a job you delegate.
- Understand that having up-to-date board policies is essential for smooth district operations.

4

Managing Conflict

There are many situations that happen in a school district that put school boards', superintendents', and district or site administrators' relationships in potential conflict. One source of conflict arises when there is not a clear understanding and written policies or protocols dealing with differences between the governance and administrative functions. When this is the case, superintendents often find themselves involved in conflict resolution activities to minimize clashes over proper roles and responsibilities.

A second subject that calls for careful monitoring and attention from the superintendent is the need for both board members and administrators to understand their legal and ethical responsibility to maintain confidentiality with respect to closed, or executive, session deliberations. Another circumstance where conflicts arise happens when board members with good intentions attempt to become involved in the day-to-day operations of the schools or attempt on-the-spot problem solving for staff members. Superintendents must also avoid surprising the board with critical and important information that should have been communicated prior to a public airing. This can lead to extreme conflict between the board and the superintendent.

Finally, when new board members are elected, their backgrounds, political sophistication, and their interests, at times, require that the superintendent develop strategies to help them become a part of an effective school district governance team and avoid allowing them to become notable as rebels in the organization.

Self-Assessment

- What is the process for ensuring that the district has a written set of protocols or policies delineating the roles and responsibilities of the board, superintendent, and other administrators?

- What is the procedure for addressing board and administrator conflict?

- How consistently does everyone—board members and the superintendent—honor the "no surprises" rule?

- What is the process for addressing breaches in confidentiality?

- How does the superintendent ensure regular board and cabinet member training sessions on state laws governing closed session and issues that are legally protected as confidential?

- How well does the superintendent understand that written communications to the board can become public documents?

- How does the superintendent monitor the relationship with the board to ensure that there is not a breakdown in communication?

WHO IS REALLY IN CHARGE?

Leaders who manage conflict best are able to draw out all parties, understanding their differing perspectives, and then find a common ideal that everyone can endorse.

—Goleman, Boyatzis, and
McKee, 2002, p. 256

As superintendents consider how to minimize conflict in the district with respect to roles and responsibilities, two basic questions arise. First, do all board members and administrators know the difference between setting policy and administering the district? Second, do site principals recognize when a board member "crosses over the line" between governance and administration? Administrators and board members must understand one another's roles and responsibilities. A clear, direct avenue for communication between the superintendent and site principals is necessary as problems arise when board members move from their policy governance role into administration.

Vignette

A young, experienced woman felt fortunate to be superintendent of a school district with eager, competent, and anxious-to-please principals. The superintendent believed in decentralized management anchored in a shared, common philosophy. Her expectation was that all employees would work in concert with the district philosophy, mission statement, and priorities. She expected the principals to model this same common philosophy and decentralized approach as they involved their employees in appropriate site-level decisions.

Although the district's five governing board members had full-time jobs, they were very involved and eager to participate in decisions, school activities, community service clubs, and volunteer work. The superintendent was not surprised when the board president asked for an agenda item that would assign each board member as a board "liaison" to a set of district schools. They would attend as many school events as possible, get the opinions of principals on board agenda items, and serve as the overall point of contact with their schools.

At the next administrative council meeting, several principals voiced their apprehension about this new school "liaison" role for board members. The superintendent said she expected a call from each principal following any board member visit. She acknowledged the principals' concerns and said she would have this topic on each of the next administrative council meeting agendas. Of course she wanted to monitor the new process, but she also saw the discussion with the principals as a way to provide them periodic training on board protocols and politics.

It wasn't long before the superintendent received calls from frustrated principals. They expressed concern that board members were acting differently and behaving, as one said, "like their boss." At the next administrative council meeting, principals asked three questions:

1. Can board members tell us what to do?

2. How do we respond when they give a directive?

3. Are board members our boss?

Clearly, the superintendent had a dilemma. The board and superintendent had adopted a new procedure that board members loved and the principals hated. Board members liked the focused involvement with particular schools but had no idea of the principals' frustration. The principals wanted to be accommodating and participatory, but they worried about who they really answered to and whose direction they should follow.

The superintendent reviewed current policies regarding board duties and responsibilities, talked to the district's legal counsel, and called a colleague superintendent to mull over the situation. She scheduled a meeting with the board president, explained the situation, and asked for advice and possible solutions. The board president, a long-time board member with a clear understanding of the distinction between policy setting and administration, suggested a special board workshop with representative principals.

Attending the special board workshop were board members, the superintendent, the cabinet members, several principals, and the district's attorney who was especially helpful in clarifying the roles of individual board members and the board as a whole. The healthy discussion that followed led to a statement of common goals, and a set of parameters that honored the roles of the board members, the superintendent, and the principals. One of the agreements that emerged from the discussion was that participation of board members at schools sites is healthy, but the superintendent retains the authority to give direction to the principals.

Analysis

This new superintendent desired to please and work harmoniously with both the board and the principals. She also believed in allowing the principals the freedom to manage their sites in a decentralized mode while expecting them to adhere to the district's philosophy, mission, and priorities. When the board suggested the liaison concept, she did not appear to anticipate the unintended consequences of board members having ties to specific schools. When principals raised concerns, the superintendent communicated her desire to monitor the process.

She failed to analyze, in-depth, the potential for role confusion inherent in this situation. She made a wise decision, however, in asking for advice from her experienced board president. Another positive step that she took was to involve the school district's attorney, a knowledgeable third party, to conduct the workshop for the board and staff. This led to a better understanding of each party's roles and responsibilities. The situation also allowed for an open discussion so that a positive agreement regarding the superintendent's authority to direct the work of the principals emerged.

Action Steps

1. Be proactive. Develop strategies to resolve conflicts that arise between the board and staff over who is really in charge.

2. Determine the extent to which board members understand their status as policymakers.

(Continued)

(Continued)

3. Work with principals on recognizing and understanding board members' desire to be involved in the schools and develop a consensus concerning meaningful participation opportunities for the board.

4. Periodically evaluate whether or not decentralization or any other model of site management the district is employing is contributing to improved student achievement and a positive educational environment for all.

NO SURPRISES

We have the problem of establishing the necessary minimum of communications so that we understand each other and can know each other's needs, goals, perceptions, and ways of doing things. Information does not supply this; only direct contact, whether by voice or written word, can communicate.

—Drucker, 1993, p. 68

The superintendent has a clear responsibility to protect the board from surprises, especially at board meetings. This is true for board members working with the superintendent as well. Prior to placing an item for action on the board agenda, the superintendent must have conducted thorough research on the history and the perceptions and expectations of the board concerning the issue.

When a matter is likely to become controversial, the superintendent must work with the district staff and other key advisers as well as the board president to ensure that there are no surprises that can result in embarrassment for the board and the district. The trust that careful planning and consistent communication with all board members engenders is immeasurable.

Vignette

In the spring of one year, staff members and the superintendent prepared for a major workshop on facilities with the architect and the construction management company who were working closely with the district facilities staff on the opening of a new school. The new school was necessary to help reduce the size of another school that was large and beyond the size the board felt appropriate. The board had promised the community that the school would open in the fall.

Despite the fact that staff had provided updates regarding delays in state and city approvals, board members continued to believe they could make their desired opening date. Five days before the facilities workshop, staff received the time lines and project lists from the architect and construction manager indicating that the school could not be completed until fall of the following school year, a full year beyond the anticipated date. Staff brought the information to the superintendent in a planning meeting. Together, they discussed how to explain to the board why the delay was a reality.

The superintendent started by speaking to the board president. Although the president was concerned about how the rest of the board would react, neither the superintendent nor the board president discussed calling the rest of the board prior to the meeting. Preparation for the workshop continued. Later, the board president called the superintendent to say she felt people were going to be upset to learn the school would not open on the date they had expected. The superintendent wondered if the president had actually talked to some of the board members, but she never confirmed this. The time line was tight to get everything ready for the meeting, so the superintendent went ahead with her preparations.

At the workshop, staff provided the schedule for construction of the new school. Board members were clearly upset. The immediate question was, "How long has staff known about this and why weren't we informed?" There was no good answer. Having assumed that the board president talked to and prepared some members, in particular the most upset member, the superintendent was caught off-guard by the reaction.

She knew the board wanted the school opened in the fall, but having not been the superintendent when the district started planning for the new school, she did not realize the depth of the board members' feelings. In addition to real concerns over the growing size of the other school, some saw it as a hot issue for the upcoming board election. The press covered the meeting and the articles in the next day's edition made the board members' unhappiness clear. Needless to say, the superintendent and the staff received numerous calls and e-mails in response to the news.

Following the workshop, the superintendent pulled staff together to look at how to resolve the problem. They contacted the architect and construction manager and shared the board members' reactions and how unacceptable this was to them. Subsequently, the superintendent called a meeting with the two board members who were most upset, key staff, and the representatives from the two companies. After brainstorming and airing of the issues, they developed a plan. It allowed for a short-term solution of a "temporary" school on the site for a fall opening class of 400 students, with a move into regular classrooms at mid-year.

(Continued)

(Continued)

> Ultimately, it all worked out well. The board was content with the partial opening of the school and the construction company owner and the architect did not compromise the quality of the new school. The superintendent, however, had to expend much time and effort focusing on rebuilding trust with some of the board members.

Analysis

The superintendent failed to take into consideration the historical context and meaning for the board of the change in the date of the opening of the school. Because this was such an important decision for the board, she and the board president should have explored in greater detail how and when the communication with all board members about the possible delay in opening the new school would occur. The depth of the board's negative reaction to a "surprise" may depend upon the magnitude of the issue, community expectations, and the strength of the trust the superintendent has with the board. The savvy superintendent provides timely and complete information even when the news is bad.

Action Steps

1. Review current district issues with staff, stressing the importance of an open dialogue concerning both the good and the bad news.

2. Develop a plan for communicating with board members about important issues or changes before they are surprised.

3. Provide your best analysis of critical issues and possible alternatives for board members in advance of suggesting changes.

4. Take time to understand each of your board member's personal and political "hot buttons."

YOU HEARD WHAT AT THE PARTY?

> *The problem with telling everything you know is that someone else is harmed. Harm may not be the intention, but it is certainly the effect.*
> —Carter, 1997, p. 54

Closed session board meetings allow the board and superintendent to discuss and deliberate about items of a confidential nature as specified by state law. These sessions have limited scope and typically include personnel issues, legal matters, union contract negotiations, and student discipline. Anything discussed in closed session is confidential and is not to be shared outside of the meeting by those attending the session. The expectation of anyone who is a participant in a closed session discussion is that all parties involved will abide by the law.

Vignette

An experienced superintendent who had just become a superintendent in a new district was faced with a breach of confidentiality by the board and staff. At her first closed session, she and the board discussed how negotiations were going with the teachers' union. The staff presented the board options on various issues and asked for direction. For the superintendent, it was a typical closed session about one of the permitted topics. What she was not prepared for was what happened next.

A few days later, a staff member came to the superintendent and said he understood that the board was about to make a specific offer to the teachers. He asked, "Where is the board getting the money to do this?" Because this staff member was not in closed session and not a member of the district's negotiating team, the superintendent asked where he had heard this information. He told her he had attended a party over the weekend and heard two board members and other staff talking about it.

The superintendent was aware that the district's former superintendent maintained a relationship with many current staff, including the business manager who had been in closed session. Both attended the weekend party, where the former superintendent asked the business manager what the board had discussed about negotiations with the teachers' union. Without thinking, the business manager told him.

Clearly, the former superintendent did not have the right to this information; but he got the information from the business manager at the party and then confronted board members as to the closed session discussion about negotiations. The former superintendent told the board he was irritated and had he still been the superintendent he would not have brought them the options they were considering. His comments led to a rather heated exchange between him and the two board members, one that was overheard by others at the party.

The new superintendent also learned that breaches of confidentiality had occurred in the past. Worse, board members and staff regularly shared information from closed session. The superintendent decided it was time to take an aggressive stance. Her first step was to

(Continued)

(Continued)

make copies of the law pertaining to closed session and call a meeting of the district management staff. She provided copies of the law, and after giving them time to read it, asked them to explain why they supposed she had wanted them to read it. Then she described what she believed they should have known—that it is totally unacceptable to share information from closed session. She explained the legal jeopardy for individuals and the district in general that can happen when confidential information becomes public. There are financial risks to the district and the possibility of lawsuits from affected employees. She concluded by informing the district management staff that there were no second chances for those violating the law. If it happened again, she would take disciplinary action. She acknowledged this was a hard line, but necessary because this behavior had to stop. All administrators understood and promised never to let it happen again.

Next, the superintendent had to tackle the second and very touchy problem of the board having violated closed session. She gave board members a heads-up by memo that she needed to talk to them about closed session confidentiality, sent them a copy of the law, and made an appointment to meet with each one. At these meetings, the superintendent and board member discussed the problems and the dangers a breach of confidentiality posed for the district. All board members also promised that they would not break confidentiality again.

Over the next few weeks, administrators and board members came to the superintendent to thank her for taking a hard line on this issue. Leaks of information had been an ongoing problem that had been ignored. Board members and staff appreciated that the superintendent confronted the issue and ultimately protected all of them and the district in general.

Analysis

The confidentiality of closed session discussions must be a core board protocol with an ongoing reemphasis on zero tolerance for violations of this commitment. When closed session discussions are shared with a wider audience, there is potential for liability, violation of employee rights, and the loss of the public's trust. The district must have a clear statement of understanding and a written commitment to the protocol that closed session discussions are indeed confidential. This superintendent took decisive action and addressed the issue of violations of closed session confidentiality with both administrators and board members in a straightforward, skillful, and timely manner.

Action Steps

1. Arrange a workshop, conducted by legal counsel, on your state's closed session law for board members and top management staff.

2. Schedule a full board discussion about the importance of maintaining confidentiality and do the same with staff. It is everyone's responsibility to police themselves to avoid harm to others and the district.

3 Clarify that each person is responsible for maintaining confidentiality.

4. Keep the board and staff updated by providing written information on changes in the confidentiality law.

5. Deal with staff breaches of closed session confidentiality with disciplinary action.

ALL INTERNAL COMMUNICATION IS NOT INTERNAL

The news media are a challenging reality in the life of most school leaders.

—Sample, 2003, p. 162

As public entities, school districts are fair game for the local news media, especially the print media. Board members are particularly sensitive about stories in the newspaper. They want to see good news in print; but as any education editor will tell you, "good news does not sell papers." Smaller- and medium-sized districts rarely can afford to employ professional public information officers or staff media officers, leaving the superintendent and board to fend for themselves.

As the public's representatives, board members want to be responsive and responsible but can be lured into making comments that do not always portray the district or a particular incident in the most favorable light. Less experienced board members or, in rare cases, rebels with other agendas can become targets for reporters requesting information that they cannot otherwise obtain because of the confidential nature of the material they are seeking. Reporters may also use the "deadline" device to catch the superintendent or a board member off-guard, calling late in the day or on Friday afternoon and saying they must have a quote. They may ask the superintendent or board member to comment on an alleged statement. If the superintendent does not comment, a typical line is, "he refused to comment." If the superintendent is unavailable, they might write, "several calls were made and the district staff failed to respond."

Vignette

A superintendent was caught off-guard, and vulnerable, when he discovered an activist board member had figured out a way to use local media to gain publicity for her causes. Her strategy was to share the superintendent's weekly communication with the reporter assigned to cover district board meetings and the schools.

At the time, the superintendent wrote about both confidential and non-confidential matters in the weekly communicator, assuming that the board would not share confidential information. One week, the superintendent wrote about an issue and mentioned this education reporter's name. The reporter was incensed and filed a public records request asking for copies of weekly communicators for two years. The superintendent called the school district's attorney for advice.

At first, the attorney suggested that the superintendent consider not sending a weekly letter, but then reasoned that if the superintendent stopped sending the weekly letter more questions would be raised. So the attorney told the superintendent to remove all confidential information (those areas covered by state law) in the weekly board communications and give the non-confidential material to the reporter. The reality for the superintendent was that the board looked forward to the weekly letter. It was an effective tool for ongoing communication and included some district information that most likely would never appear on a board agenda.

Over the next few weeks, the superintendent talked to each board member about the fact that someone shared confidential information with the local reporter. The superintendent conveyed his concern and disappointment without identifying the culprit. He also alerted the entire board to the hazards of sharing confidential information.

Although the reporter never picked up the requested material, the superintendent learned the reality of sage advice he had heard from a colleague: Leaders should never write or say anything they would not want to see on the front page of the newspaper. No question, the superintendent learned a valuable lesson about careful communication.

The superintendent decided to continue the weekly correspondence on white paper, but changed the format of the letter and supporting documents, weighed every word he wrote, and divided it into several topics. The headings he used were: The Superintendent's Week, Board Follow-up, Good News About Our Schools, and Weekly Correspondence, which included invitations. Under separate cover and using blue paper, he sent "Confidential Matters," only those specified by state law that board members could discuss in closed session.

Analysis

The superintendent made an assumption about board members' loyalty to the school district and its mission. He did not recognize that some board members' political or personal agendas shape their board service in ways that at times can prove harmful to the district. The decision to speak to each board member about the situation and avoid the disruption that too much attention to this matter might cause was wise for the time. The superintendent recognized the need to contact the school district's attorney for assistance in thinking through options. Restructuring his weekly letter to the board was a positive outcome.

Superintendents must recognize that media representatives believe they have a right and duty to protect and inform the public, and may do so in ways that are not always pleasant. This superintendent learned that some will co-opt individual board members to gain access to confidential district information if they can. As the chief school administrator, the superintendent has an obligation to develop the knowledge and skills to deal with media representatives in an effective manner and to protect district information that is legally confidential. The board expects it and the community deserves a superintendent who works with the media in a way that brings respect to the district and its stakeholders.

Action Steps

1. Exercise caution in writing internal correspondence. You do not know when a board member will have a reason to share confidential information with a newspaper reporter or someone in the community.

2. Have the board appoint a board spokesperson, often the president or chair.

3. Prepare factual summaries of incidents for the media, but make sure the board has the information first.

4. Call your school district's attorney for advice when a media representative asks for information that you believe is legally protected.

RESPONDING TO A VIOLATION OF BOARD PROTOCOL

In human systems, structure includes how people make decisions—"operating policies" whereby we translate perceptions, goals, rules, and norms into actions.

—Senge, 1990, p. 40

Effective board-superintendent teams are a result of creating agreements, often called protocols, on how to work together. These teams discuss how to handle situations that face them and what role each should play. To continue building their effectiveness, many board members evaluate themselves each year, with a major part of the self-evaluation focused on how they carry out their roles and conduct themselves as members of the governance team. Members may pose such questions as: Have they followed their own protocols? If a protocol is violated, how is this brought forward and addressed by the entire team?

Vignette

For two years, the board and superintendent worked diligently with a facilitator to develop and revise protocols to clarify their roles and guide their behavior as board members and superintendent. At the end of the process, they unanimously agreed to the set of protocols they developed.

A few weeks later, a board member visited a school where she talked to a student teacher, and then she violated one of these newly adopted protocols. The teacher told the board member he did not have adequate furniture in his classroom to conduct the lessons he planned and shared his frustration about trying to get the furniture for his classroom. In her desire to be supportive of this teacher, the board member walked to the school's front office and called the director of operations, demanding that he deliver the requested furniture to this classroom immediately. The director felt he was in a difficult position and called his supervisor, who told him to do his best to respond to the board member's request.

The next day, while reading her e-mail, the superintendent learned of the incident. Surprised and disturbed by the board member's behavior, she called and asked to meet with her immediately. The board member knew the reason for the call and apologized saying, "I know I was bad, but I needed to solve the situation for this wonderful teacher."

When the two met the next day, they discussed the board member's behavior and why it was a problem for the organization. The superintendent explained that every day every person in every department had priorities. Just because the board member saw a need at one school in one classroom at one moment, it did not mean it suddenly became the highest priority for the district. With 60 schools in the district, all board members must understand that support staff members are working hard to respond to many priorities on a daily basis.

The superintendent and board member reviewed the appropriate protocol that stated if a board member encountered a problem at a school he or she was to direct the concern to the principal. If there was a concern that could not be solved at the school level, the member could share the information with the superintendent by e-mail or telephone call.

The involved board member was a first-term, well-intentioned board member who knew she had violated a board agreement and was very apologetic. She and the superintendent agreed to share this experience with the entire board as a reminder of how easy it is as a board member to use your position inappropriately.

Prior to discussing the issue with the entire board, the board member individually told each of her four colleagues what she had done and apologized for violating the board's agreement. The discussion that followed at the next quarterly board retreat was invaluable and provided an opportunity for veteran board members to share stories about times when they encountered similar situations and ways they learned to respond effectively.

Although the other board members acknowledged that she had violated a board protocol, they did not censure this board member but rather used the opportunity to reinforce among and between themselves how important it is to have protocols and abide by them. The board member still takes some light-hearted teasing about the incident, but the entire team recognizes that bringing the incident forward was a learning experience and a good reminder for everyone.

Analysis

The superintendent's confidence and skill helped to reinforce an important concept concerning violation of a board protocol. Her sensitive yet pointed discussion with the offending board member helped set the stage for the board to discuss how it had handled similar situations in the past. This incident allowed them to take the recent experience of a board member as a reminder to respect their agreements. If the superintendent had not dealt with the matter immediately and directly, there was the potential for an even more egregious breach of protocol in the future.

Action Steps

1. Work with the board to develop protocols that all members will agree to abide by. Expect everyone to be held to the same agreements.

2. Understand that it is common for new board members, who are often unprepared for the pressure they feel to solve problems, to violate a board protocol by responding to complaints brought to them in their new role.

(Continued)

(Continued)

3. Do not ignore the violation of a protocol. Ignoring a violation can cause dissention among the entire board team.

4. Build regular retreats with the board into the calendar.

5. Make a review of board protocols a part of the agenda at least once a year.

THE REBEL BOARD MEMBER

Civility involves the discipline of our passions for the sake of living a common life with others.

—Carter, 1998, p. 109

After a few years and a few board elections, most superintendents experience a rebel board member or two. Some are overtly rebellious, others more covert. These people tend not to accept their role as policymakers and community representatives, but seem to want to go their own way. Often they display little or no respect for the rights and feelings of staff or their fellow board members. A rebel board member can upset the balance in the organization by forcing the superintendent to play firefighter. The overt rebel sometimes finds his behavior tempered by the public. The covert rebel, however, who relishes gossip, rumor, and innuendo, can cause havoc in the school district.

Eventually, the superintendent must deal with this individual board member. Either intervening or allowing the situation to continue can put the superintendent in an awkward position with other board members who typically do not wish to deal with dysfunction on the board. If the issue is not dealt with, the superintendent's tenure in the district is threatened, and sometimes administrators who are affected by the rebel's behavior begin to leave the system. Superintendents seek to understand the reasons for the behavior and then find ways to minimize the damage. They must find the right ways and time to involve the rest of the board and to confront the offending board member.

Vignette

A new member joined the school board after low voter turnout in a relatively quiet election put her in the place of a two-term incumbent. At the time, people knew very little about her. Later, she told the superintendent she had not expected to win, but won because the incumbent was "too lazy to campaign." The superintendent discovered the new board member, the "rebel," was a high school dropout and active in numerous social movements. She told the superintendent that her interest was in making sure that her issues were important in the school district.

More disconcerting, the superintendent learned this new trustee attended seminars on how to disrupt public meetings, obtain publicity, and embarrass her opponents. She also discovered the rebel disliked those she termed "ultra-religious people" or people she deemed "rich." Within a short time of her election, the rebel set out to find a person in every school to give her any unfavorable information about the principal or someone on the staff. Her goal was to see the superintendent's reaction when she forwarded the negative information, asking her to do something. The superintendent recognized that this could not go on without substantial disruption to the system. She also recognized that, as an elected official, this board member had some credibility in the community.

The superintendent instituted four strategies to improve the situation. First, she asked another board member to help bring this rebel into the system. Second, the superintendent instituted a monthly lunch during which the superintendent, the rebel, and the experienced board member talked about their families and shared good news about the schools. A third strategy was to have the rebel visit schools with a more positive board member. Finally, the superintendent made a habit of talking to principals about how to deal with board members in an upbeat way no matter what they thought about them.

After a few months, the rebel's calls to the superintendent criticizing principals for their handling of matters began to diminish. Each time the rebel visited a school, the principal went overboard to welcome her, show her around the school, and give her an information packet, a sweatshirt, a pin, or some other memento. The rebel was so impressed by the principals' kindness that she became more open with the superintendent. The superintendent also remembered to call principals individually and thank them for the courtesy extended to board members.

The superintendent talked to the rebel about her philosophy and her experiences, and how important it was to have the support for the schools from all board members. She told her about a commercial that featured a man saying, "Stay within the lines, the lines are your friends." The superintendent conceded that she might, at times, become too rigid in her law- and rule-abiding attitude and behavior, but that it served her well.

Later, at times when the rebel board member started moving outside the bounds of acceptable and agreed-upon board member protocols, the superintendent reminded her of their conversation about "staying within the lines." The rebel actually laughed and

(Continued)

(Continued)

thanked the superintendent for her wise counsel. Upon reflection, the superintendent concluded that this board member became a rebel because her training and experience as social activist taught her not to trust the system. The only option for the superintendent was to find ways to help the rebel develop trust in the district and the district's staff so the important work of educating students was not disrupted by having administrators spend time chasing rumors started by this board member.

Analysis

With every board election, there is a new set of factors related to board members' philosophies, beliefs, and styles. The profiles of board members differ. When one board member demonstrates a more "individualistic" personal agenda, it is a wise superintendent that observes and documents specific examples of behaviors that are contrary to the board's primary mission of being a policy-making body. When behaviors negatively impact progress and interfere with relationships, it is important to address the actions openly and honestly with respect and collegiality. The superintendent did not allow the board member to continue along a negative path. She developed a strategy involving another board member as well as the principals. This action helped to bring the board member into the system that she was elected to help govern.

Action Steps

1. Just as it takes time to develop a new employee or correct an errant employee, it takes time, understanding, and work to turn a rebel board member into a positive contributor. Analyze your situation, and develop a strategy for working with a rebel board member.

2. Enlist the assistance of another board member to work with you and the rebel, but also refrain from gossiping about one board member to another.

3. Stay positive. Model the behavior you want to have your administrative team adopt when dealing with all board members.

4. Thank administrators for showing board members around their schools. Thank the board members for visiting campuses.

5. Just as we do not choose our students or parents, we do not choose our board members; however, honor their work and make them the best they can be.

CHAPTER SUMMARY

The superintendent has a responsibility for establishing a climate and processes that minimize conflicts so that the real work of the district can move forward. Without written protocols or policies clearly delineating the roles and responsibilities of the board and the administrative staff, conflicts can arise requiring the superintendent's attention. Breaches in confidentiality have the potential for conflict as well. Board members and the administrative staff need periodic updates on state laws regarding issues that are confidential and can be discussed in closed session. The superintendent and staff must adhere to the "no surprises" rule in communicating important information to the board. Finally, the different backgrounds and points of view that board members represent dictate that the superintendent help each board member become a part of an effective governance team.

Superintendents are catalysts for managing interpersonal conflicts so that the important work of providing an excellent school system for students can move forward.

Key Strategies

- Lead the board in establishing protocols specifying roles and responsibilities of board members and the administrative staff.
- Establish avenues for administrators to seek resolution when they become involved in conflicts with the board or an individual board member.
- Provide regular training sessions on state confidentiality laws.
- Deal with violations of confidentiality laws directly to protect individuals and the district.
- Work with administrators to find ways for board members to become meaningfully involved with the schools to minimize crossing the line between governance and administration.
- Communicate with board members about important issues impacting their decisions in a timely, accurate, and thoroughly researched manner so that there are no preventable surprises.
- Determine each board member's interests, concerns, and "hot button issues."
- Assume responsibility for sensitive, open, and honest communication with board members who violate board-approved protocols.
- Prepare internal communication between the board and superintendent with care, recognizing that any written communication with the board has the potential of being shared with the media.
- Take responsibility for developing the knowledge and skills to deal with the media in ways that project a cooperative and positive image of the district.
- Work with all board members, even the rebels, to help them become positive, contributing members of the governance team.

5

Moving On and Succession Planning

An issue superintendents all face, but rarely think about, is when to leave a district. This can be either to move to another district, leave the profession for another job, or, ultimately, to retire. Regardless of the reasons superintendents move on or retire, the way superintendents leave is critical to the health of the organization. In terms of the board, staff, and community, superintendents have a responsibility to say good-bye in a sensitive and positive manner and to make sure a successful transition occurs with the new superintendent, even when leaving is not the departing superintendent's decision.

When board members know superintendents are leaving, they may request suggestions on how to select the next superintendent. If this happens, superintendents need to be prepared to handle this and decide whether or not they should or want to be involved.

When deciding to move to another district, superintendents need to prepare just as though it was their first superintendency. They must use techniques to find the right district that matches their background of training, experiences, and personal talents, thus preparing them for future success.

Looking at options for retirement, superintendents have many choices, including various consulting jobs, working at a college or university, serving as an interim superintendent, or leaving the profession entirely. The key is thinking about each option and making informed decisions.

Self-Assessment

- Who do you need to tell of your plans to retire, and in what order?

- Even if you are a very private person, what is the value of a public retirement event?

- What should your role be, if any, in the selection of your successor?

- What are some jobs that interest you and that you might like to pursue?

- How do you go about finding a new district that is right for you?

- What do you need to do if you want to be an interim superintendent?

WHEN TO LEAVE

When positive board-superintendent relationships are slipping, the whole district suffers and students and staff live with the negative consequences.

—Kimball, 2005, p. 6

Board members and superintendents tend to have strong egos and personalities. When the superintendent's relationships with board members deteriorate, superintendents need to assess what impact that is having on their performance and the rest of the district.

Relationships between the superintendent and board members may be so strained that the only decision the superintendent can make is to leave the district, and either to go to another district, retire, or leave the profession altogether.

Vignette

During a superintendent's first year in the district, a new board member was elected. The relationship was strong in the beginning. They had similar backgrounds, having both been social science teachers and being relatively close in age. Although the superintendent heard from a few people in the community that this new

(Continued)

(Continued)

member could be difficult, this was not evident at the start. A major personnel matter changed the relationship.

A middle school clerk was alleged to be using school funds to purchase some personal items. The school's principal had come upon some records that pointed to this and brought the information to the chief business officer. The superintendent, business officer, and principal met and agreed an investigation was necessary and proceeded to gather more evidence. The superintendent informed board members about the investigation; however, the superintendent was not fully aware of the popularity of the clerk with the school staff and parents or existing concerns some board members had about the effectiveness of the principal.

The board member, with whom the superintendent had so much in common, turned on the superintendent. District staff, after the superintendent's consultation with legal counsel, dealt with the clerk, confronting her with the evidence. Next the superintendent had to face dealing with the changed relationship with the board member.

The clerk resigned and, frankly, all hell broke loose. "She could not have done these things," was the oft-repeated statement by many district staff members who knew the long-employed clerk. The clerk was out in the community bad-mouthing district leadership, ignoring the incriminating evidence, and "playing the victim."

Despite the evidence, the one board member would not back off. She accused the superintendent of lying and saying the principal fabricated the situation. The board member accused the superintendent of blindly supporting the principal and believing the false charges. The rest of the board was supportive of the superintendent's actions, but would not confront the board member when she continued to attack the superintendent and staff.

Over the next two years, the board member grew increasingly difficult. She went behind the superintendent's back and that of the board's to talk with the unions, and, generally, made life miserable for the superintendent.

The superintendent was able to maintain a good relationship with the rest of the board and was well respected in the district and throughout the community. By the end of the second year, however, it became evident to the superintendent that staying in the district with this board member was not an option. The negativity was wearing on the superintendent and creating stress among the other board members. Even staff members who were not close to the situation were feeling the fallout of the problems and tension. Because she cared about the district, the superintendent decided to seek another position and ultimately left the district.

Analysis

In trying to solve a personnel matter, the superintendent did not gather enough information about the players prior to moving forward with her plan. The superintendent was not aware that there were concerns about the principal, the level of staff support for the clerk, nor the relationship the clerk had with one of the board members. By not checking this out first, the superintendent proceeded in a manner that created a situation that was difficult for the whole board and for herself. She had to deal with the issue, but might have taken a different, more methodical approach, laying the groundwork for the right outcome.

Once the damage was done, it was difficult for the superintendent to undo it. She recognized the impact the negative relationship with one board member was having on the organization and made the choice to leave. If constant negativity is causing problems for a superintendent, a board, or a district, leaving may well be the best choice.

Action Steps

1. Understand relationships that exist between staff and board members prior to taking action on personnel matters.

2. Analyze your own behavior as a superintendent to see how it may contribute to escalating an issue.

3. Determine the impact a negative relationship has on the climate of the district and whether staying or leaving will improve the future of the district and your own effectiveness.

LEARNING ABOUT A NEW DISTRICT

Researching a potential new community and school district can be a wonderful adventure.

—Johnston et al., 2002, p. 2

Researching a new school district and community will help you determine if the district you are considering is right for you. There are many ways to do this. No matter what way you select, it is critical that you have a plan, be thorough in your research, and be willing to look critically at what you find out.

Vignette

Upon reading about a superintendent position in a statewide listing of job opportunities, the superintendent called the search firm and obtained the brochure describing the geographical setting of the community, the demographic data of the school district, and the qualifications board members were looking for in their new superintendent.

Based on the description in the brochure and what the superintendent already knew about the district and community, she began to make a list of what skills and experiences the board members wanted in their new superintendent and compare this to her background. She listed every activity in which she had experience related to each item.

Once she had completed this task and determined she had the skills and experiences the board desired, she began her research of the community and district. Her first step was to have the local newspaper delivered to her home so she could learn about the district and the school board and see what themes emerged.

The superintendent then spent several weekends visiting the community and talking with community members and students about the schools. She obtained a map of the district and on her weekend visits walked every school site and peeked in classroom windows. At each school site, she jotted down her observations. She continued her research by calling the local chamber of commerce and asking for a packet of materials for visitors or individuals inquiring about business opportunities, and she stopped by the city offices to pick up materials about the schools. Real estate offices were next on her list. At each of her stops, she recorded the comments she heard about the district.

The superintendent scheduled an interview with the county superintendent of schools to ask some in-depth questions about the fiscal soundness of the district and its reputation. To receive more specific detail about the district's budgetary priorities, she called a professional organization that gathers data about financial expenditures for each district in the state.

The superintendent requested and received from the district a packet of detailed materials, including copies of the school profiles, an employee directory, school newsletters, a report listing student performance data for the past several years, copies of union contracts, copies of board agendas, the last budget approved by the board, and a brochure about the education foundation.

After collecting all this data, organizing and analyzing it, and comparing it to her skills and experiences, she determined that this district was a good match for her. She moved ahead with the process. She sent in her application, interviewed for the position, and, ultimately, was hired as the new superintendent.

Analysis

Searching for your first or next superintendency can be daunting. If you have a plan for how to do this and follow it, you will be able to find a position that should be right for you. The plan should include visits, if possible, reading budgets, board minutes and newspapers, and talking to people who know about the district. Thorough research will help you determine whether this is the right fit for you and the district.

Action Steps

1. Have a specific plan on how to research a district and community.

2. Keep lists of what you learn about the district and what the board is looking for in a new superintendent and compare your skills and experiences to this list.

3. Talk to as many people as possible about the district, including students, county superintendents, community members, local business owners, representatives of the chamber of commerce, real estate agents, and others depending on the district.

KNOWING WHEN TO RETIRE

Don't think of retiring from the world until the world will be sorry that you retire.

—Samuel Johnson, quoted in Safire and Safir, 1992, p. 305

Many superintendents fill their lives so full with their work they have a difficult time determining when it is the right time to retire. Sometimes, they base their decision on their age, the number of years they have in the retirement system, the income they need, their health, their relationship with their board, or their family needs.

Asking other superintendents how they made their decision is one way to learn what others have done, but the final decision is a very personal one. It is also a very difficult one.

Vignette

A superintendent in her 12th year of service attended a meeting of practicing and retired superintendents. She announced she was considering retirement and asked if some of the retired superintendents

(Continued)

(Continued)

would give advice based on their own experiences making the decision.

The retirees started by asking some good-humored questions about the decision: Are you old enough to be the parent of your board members? Are you falling asleep at board meetings that go beyond 9:30 p.m.? Does it seem that issues about public education keep cycling around every decade? Are you counting how many board meetings you have attended in your career or how many you would have left if you set a retirement date?

They went on to offer advice on personal topics, such as make sure you are financially prepared; have your arrangements for your medical and dental insurance, and perhaps long-term care insurance in place; consider what your spouse thinks and how he or she will respond and discuss possible changes in roles and responsibilities; set up an office at home and don't expect your spouse to be your secretary, book your appointments, or make your travel arrangements; and, of course, don't go back to the district office and try to fix things after you are gone.

The conversation moved on to the more serious subject of when to make the announcement. They agreed it should not be too early or too late, and the consensus was between three and six months was right for the board and staff. Once a retirement is announced, the superintendent can become a lame duck, making it more difficult to engage staff and the community in new initiatives. They also suggested that, when possible, have time remaining on your contract to prevent rumors about why you are leaving.

After giving advice about advance planning, the group of colleagues returned to the big question that started the conversation: "How will I know when it is time?" The consensus was: "You'll just know. It will come together and you will know the time is right." One of the first clues will be when you make an appointment with a retirement consultant and consider the amount of your income. A second will be when you wake up in the morning and are not excited about going to work. A third is when you realize the relationship with your board is not working as well as you would like and yet you don't want to move to another superintendency. The retired superintendents concluded that it is a very individual decision. They encouraged superintendents to talk with others, and then do their homework about their own needs and desires.

Analysis

Although common issues exist for superintendents considering retirement, there is no one right answer. Superintendents need to decide if it is the right time for them and if they are able handle the changes in their life that will take place. All must identify their individual needs, such as finances and insurance. Additionally, thought needs to be given to the status of the district and the timing of leaving.

Action Steps

1. Before deciding to retire, think through plans very carefully; health, financial, and social considerations all play a part in the decision.

2. Tell the board of your decision to retire.

3. Consider the appropriate date to announce your retirement and how it will impact you and the district.

4. Write your resignation letter in a thoughtful and considerate manner. Even if you have differences with the board, credit them for their many accomplishments.

SAYING GOOD-BYE

You know, I never have much trouble playing a part. The real challenge is getting on stage—and then getting off. . . . Always leave them wanting more.

—Frank, 1986, p. 96

When school boards hire a superintendent, they tend to express concern about how many years the superintendent anticipates staying with the district because they recognize that the stability of the district is compromised if the person in the superintendent's position is replaced too often. Boards often experience difficulty, as well as the staff and community, if they believe the superintendent left the district over disagreements with the board or when circumstances in another district made it more attractive for their superintendent to leave.

The least controversial situation for a board occurs when superintendents decide to retire from districts. Retirements allow the boards and communities to bring closure to their association, implement a search process, and move forward to develop a consensus about the qualities they desire in the new superintendent. Even when there are differences between boards and superintendents, how superintendents choose to retire can affect their future and the future of the district.

Vignette

Although the superintendent in a suburban district felt healthy and productive, she believed some board members were unhappy with her performance and her perceived power in the community. Her position in the community as a long-time resident and recognized leader in several important organizations made it somewhat difficult for them to fire her or not renew her contract.

The difficulties for the superintendent started when none of the board members held a full-time job. Two were housewives and three had been retired for several years. Each board member began to make individual appointments with the superintendent asking for action on their favorite projects. Two members constantly asked the superintendent to intervene in situations involving other board members with whom they had disagreements. No matter how much information the superintendent gave them, it was never enough, particularly for the three retired board members who wanted notification of the most trivial incidents.

In closed session, about four months before the end of the school term, the superintendent notified the board, by letter and orally, of her decision to retire. The superintendent's letter gave board members credit for their many accomplishments and sincere gratitude for allowing her to serve the children of the community in a variety of roles. The board accepted the resignation with grace.

A committee of seven administrators, including elementary and secondary principals, district directors, and administrative assistants, planned two retirement celebrations for the superintendent. They selected the local country club for a formal dinner celebration and invited the staff, politicians, service club presidents, chamber of commerce officers, college and university officials, law enforcement administrators, the district attorney, union leaders, parent and community leaders, and superintendents from other local districts. The second event was for district teachers and classified employees, who attended an afternoon reception held in the district's boardroom.

At the high school awards ceremonies in June, student board members presented plaques to the superintendent recognizing her service. Although all this attention felt uncomfortable at times, these events helped the district and community achieve closure with this superintendent's administration and set the stage for the transition to a new superintendent.

Analysis

Leaving the superintendency is a complicated process. There are many steps to think through and many people to consider. Sharing with the board first, before the announcement is made public, provides board members with the opportunity to prepare what they will say to the public. This is a hard time for most superintendents and one they struggle with internally. They have given their all to the work, and the emotions that come with leaving are complex.

Even those superintendents who do not like the limelight need to understand what their retirement means to others, and allow events to honor them. Many people in districts want to say good-bye. In addition, orderly transition from one leader to another should become part of the district tradition and culture.

Action Steps

1. Consider all the stakeholders and their needs in saying good-bye.

2. Understand the ongoing district culture and traditions.

3. Allow the staff and community to say good-bye in the way they choose—with your input and limits. At times, you will feel that they are overdoing things, but allow them to show their gratitude and respect for your efforts in their own manner.

MAKING THE TRANSITION

I've had my time and it was lovely. And I'm grateful for it. But now I move over and make room for somebody else.
——Barbara Stanwyck, quoted in Safire
and Safir, 1992, p. 305

Community members, board members, and staff have the tendency to want things the way they were and may try to involve the retired superintendent in what is going on within the district after he or she leaves. When superintendents stay within the communities in which they worked, they have to be careful not to let this happen.

Superintendents may want to find ways to stay involved in their communities without staying involved in the district. When they retire, they need to think about how they will handle their new role within the community. Superintendents also need to consider how much time they want to commit and how much time they need for a good balance in their lives.

Vignette

The former superintendent resigned from several community boards to allow the organizations to invite the new superintendent to be a member. The superintendent did this because she knew the importance of helping the community recognize and respect the new superintendent. For a solid year after retirement, it seemed that everywhere she turned people in the community greeted her warmly and asked how she enjoyed retirement. They said she looked rested and they were happy for her. High school students working at local stores and restaurants also recognized the superintendent and asked how she enjoyed retirement.

As time went on, people in the community and some staff members began their conversations with such comments as "We are happy for you, but we miss you. It's just not the same." The retired superintendent sensed that perhaps the family's decision to remain in the community had not been the best, but, at this point, her spouse wanted to stay with family and friends. She decided it was time to be less visible and do other things. She accepted interim superintendent assignments and positions on three new boards including the board of a local college foundation.

Other opportunities for volunteering arose constantly; however, she decided that she valued balance in her life. Her decision was to accept limited work assignments, volunteer on boards where she felt she could make a contribution because of her background in education, and travel to places that were restful rather than reminiscent of the hectic sightseeing travels of her younger years.

Analysis

It is important to consider how you will handle the situation when the new superintendent takes over. The temptation to be drawn back into the district environment will be there, but new superintendents deserve the opportunity to make the district theirs. It is best if the retiring superintendent engages in new activities within the community that are unrelated to those in which he or she once participated. In addition, the superintendent has to be careful about over-committing and filling in all available time. In that case, it leaves one wondering why the superintendent retired.

Action Steps

1. Decide whether or not you will remain in the community where you were superintendent.

2. Consider the organizations you belong to. Which should you continue and which should you resign from?

3. Assume control of your newfound freedom. People value your expertise, but you need to decide how you will spend your time.

SELECTING A NEW SUPERINTENDENT

The number of potential approaches to achieve an objective is unlimited. There are as many as your imagination will allow. But just as you should have only one clear-cut objective, so you must choose only one approach.

—Frank, 1986, p. 35

Boards sometimes look to the leaving superintendent, especially if the superintendent is well liked by the board, for guidance in selecting the new superintendent. As in all matters, superintendents need to consider what their appropriate role in the process should be. Outgoing superintendents should consider the expertise required for a task and assess whether they are the best qualified to assist the board with this critical decision. Selection of the new superintendent is one of, if not the most, critical jobs a board has.

Vignette

When the board asked the retiring superintendent for her opinion, she recommended several options for selecting a new superintendent. These included hiring an outside consulting firm, using the county Office of Education, or doing the search using district staff. By consensus, the board members decided not to hire a search firm or use the county Office of Education. They felt that it was not worth the money because their two previous searches resulted in inside candidates being selected.

The board asked the superintendent to draft a recruitment letter for the board president's signature and send it to all the superintendents in a two-county area. The superintendent's staff mailed more than 50 letters to local school districts. Board members also requested that the superintendent send a letter to employee and parent groups and the local newspaper asking for opinions about desirable characteristics for a new superintendent. Thus, the current superintendent served as the search consultant for her replacement.

(Continued)

(Continued)

> Opinions derived from surveying the staff and community formed the basis for some of the questions board members used during their interview process. They asked the superintendent and her cabinet to suggest potential questions as well. The human resources staff compiled the questions and the current superintendent selected and recommended a final set of questions for the board.
>
> Although there was somewhat of an undercurrent of resentment because some in the community blamed the board for the superintendent's decision to retire, the board respected the superintendent's abilities and accepted the recommended set of questions without modification. Fewer candidates than anticipated applied. This situation was somewhat confounding to two board members, but comforting for three who preferred an inside candidate. When the final candidate selection ended, the board interviewed six people, all of whom were current assistant or deputy superintendents from within and from surrounding districts. The one inside candidate won the board's approval on a 3-to-2 vote.

Analysis

Boards have many options when hiring a new superintendent. Most choose a professional search firm, which separates the departing superintendent from the process. In this case, board members did not, preferring to use the current superintendent because of their trust and community support for her. It is unusual for superintendents to be part of the process to pick their successor, and they need to be cognizant of problems that could arise such as the split decision on a new leader.

Action Steps

1. Help the board members see the pros and cons of conducting their own search and of using a consulting firm with expertise in searches.

2. Consider the ramifications of the superintendent helping to select his or her successor.

WORKING AS AN INTERIM SUPERINTENDENT

> *The right interim superintendent at just the right juncture can bring respite to a troubled district, focus to a chaotic one, and unity to a divided one.*
>
> —Ramsey, 2000, p. 26

If a superintendent decides to continue working after retirement, there are many professional opportunities. Each person must decide what type of work he or she wants to do and how to start the process of finding full- or part-time work. Becoming an interim superintendent is one way to stay involved in education but not at the same pace as being a long-term superintendent.

Vignette

A superintendent retired in her mid-fifties after 14 years of being a superintendent in two districts. She had decided not to work but found after a year that she missed the stimulation of being with people and considered being an interim superintendent a good way of having the best of both worlds.

To begin the process of finding an interim position, she let her professional associations know of her interest, and she contacted a few regional offices of education as well as a few of her superintendent friends. She also made decisions about how far away from her home she would be willing to work, what kind of contract she would need, how she wished to be paid, and what she felt would be appropriate compensation. Within a short time, she started to receive phone calls letting her know which districts were looking for interims and offers of referrals.

The first district that contacted her did not work out. A few weeks later, however, she received another call for an interim superintendent position, had an interview with the board, and was hired that same day.

In negotiating an interim contract, she had several considerations. Did she want to be an employee of the district or an independent contractor? Did she want to have a long buyout period or just a few days if it did not work out with the board members? How would they determine her pay and what benefits would she receive, if any? How long was the contract? What were the board members' expectations?

She knew it was important to be clear about expectations before signing the contract. The longer her contract, she knew, the more she would be expected to become part of the community and make recommendations that would affect the future. And, the longer she stayed, the more the board and staff would rely on her.

She chose to be hired as an independent contractor for three months, but ended up staying for 10 months until the board hired the new superintendent. Board members delayed the hiring process so that they could have the interim superintendent work through some difficulties the district was having with the community.

(Continued)

(Continued)

> The board also had the interim superintendent work a few weeks after the new superintendent came on board, so she could share with the new superintendent what was going on in the district. This gave the new superintendent the ability to learn about the district and board in a shorter amount of time.

Analysis

Serving as an interim superintendent can be rewarding. You are able to provide support to an organization in transition and, at the same time, provide yourself with the satisfaction of staying involved in education and doing something you enjoy. As an interim, you know that you will be leaving at a certain time. This gives you the freedom to provide the board with an honest assessment of the district, staff, and board relationships. You are also able to provide other perspectives on issues based on your experience and offer to help the district move forward past a difficult time.

As you finish your interim experience, you should provide the board and new superintendent a summary of what you did while there. It should be confidential and include what you accomplished, what you were not able to accomplish, and suggestions for the future, leaving it up to the board members to decide what they want to do with this information.

Action Steps

1. Contact appropriate groups to indicate an interest in this kind of work.

2. Determine personal/professional criteria, such as location, salary, and so on for accepting the interim position.

3. Understand how to negotiate a contract with a board of education.

4. When completing the position, provide written documentation of accomplishments and future needs.

CHAPTER SUMMARY

Moving on can be difficult for superintendents, especially if it is not their choice. How superintendents handle their departure is important for them and for the district. Learning what options are available to them and how to access these options will help make the transition easier, whether it involves a new district, a job outside of education, or retirement.

Key Strategies

- When making recommendations related to personnel, make sure all interrelationships between the people affected are considered: board members, employees, staff, and community. Without this information, the recommendation could have an unintended outcome.
- Having a plan before searching for a new superintendency will help the search be successful. Make a plan and then follow it. If things are discovered about the district or board that don't match your background and experience as superintendent, do not continue this search but move the search to another district until the right one is found.
- When planning on retiring, check into health insurance benefits, retirement income, and so on. Consider what will happen after retirement.
- When leaving the district, either to retire or to move to another district, tell the board members first so they are prepared for the questions they will receive from staff and community members.
- Let the staff and community celebrate the superintendent's leaving. This gives closure to the superintendent and to them. After the celebration, move on to the next adventure, whether it is retiring and staying in the community, moving to a new district, or taking on a new responsibility.
- Negative board-superintendent relationships hurt both the district and superintendent. When this happens, leave. Take control of the process and work with the board for a good transition.
- Determine the appropriate role the current superintendent should play in helping the board to find the new superintendent.
- When looking for an interim superintendency, contact appropriate groups to indicate interest; determine personal/professional criteria, such as location, salary, and so on; and negotiate a contract that works.

Resource A

Board–Superintendent Protocols
for Effective Governance

PURPOSE

The board of trustees is the educational policy-making body for the district. To effectively meet the district's challenges, the board and superintendent must function together as a leadership team. To ensure unity among team members, effective protocols—operating procedures—must be in place. There are general protocols for the board and superintendent, as well as some specifically for the board, and still others for the superintendent.

As Members of the Board and as Superintendent, We Will

1. Keep teaching and learning as the primary focus of our work.

2. Value, respect, and support public education.

3. Model good learning by participating in professional development.

4. Respect the differences between governance and management.

5. Recognize and respect differences of perspective and style on the board and among staff, students, parents, and the community.

6. Operate with trust and integrity.

7. Keep confidential matters confidential.

AUTHORS' NOTE: This *sample* set of protocols focuses on leadership, governance, and management, as opposed to board meetings per se. We recommend the board-superintendent team work together to develop a set of protocols such as these and put them in place before developing, again together, the actual board meeting protocols. These are samples only. State school board associations have samples as do many school districts across the nation, and many can be accessed via district Web sites.

As a Board, We Will

1. Understand that the authority of the board rests with the board as a whole and not with individual board members.

2. Define the district's core values and beliefs.

3. Develop with the superintendent a vision of a district with high-performing students and staff.

4. Establish clear expectations for student success that promote equity of outcomes for all students.

5. Establish a structure that moves the district toward achievement of its vision, mission, and strategic goals. This structure is established through the board's policy-making and policy-review functions.

6. Make sure the agenda and behaviors reflect the district's core values and beliefs.

7. Govern in a dignified and professional manner, treating everyone with civility and respect.

8. Take collective responsibility for the board's performance.

9. Evaluate on a regular basis the board's effectiveness against a predetermined set of criteria.

10. Ensure there are opportunities for the diverse range of opinions and beliefs in the community to inform the board.

11. Involve the community, parents, students, and staff in developing a shared vision of district success that focuses on the progress all students and staff make toward meeting high standards.

12. Adopt, evaluate, and update policies that enable the district to achieve its vision, mission, and strategic goals.

13. Adopt a budget that supports achievement of vision and mission and monitor on a regular basis the fiscal health of the district.

14. Establish a framework for collective bargaining that supports high-quality teaching and learning.

15. Ensure that the district operates within the legal parameters established by local, state, and federal government agencies.

To Build a Strong Superintendent-Board Leadership Team, the Board Will

1. Hire and support a superintendent who will strive to achieve the district's vision, mission, and goals.

2. Establish with the superintendent strategic goals that anticipate changes in the internal and external environments and reflect a commitment to continuous improvement.

3. Conduct regular and timely evaluations of the superintendent based on agreed-upon goals, established board directions, and district performance.

4. Commit time to building a team approach to governance based on open, honest communication.

As Superintendent, I Will

1. Work toward creating a team with the board dedicated to students.

2. Respect and acknowledge the board's role in setting policy and overseeing the performance of the superintendent.

3. Work with the board to establish a clear vision for the school district.

4. Communicate the common vision.

5. Recognize that the board-superintendent governance relationship requires support by the district's management team.

6. Understand the distinction between board and staff roles, and respect the role of the board as the representative of the community.

7. Accept leadership responsibility and be accountable for implementing the vision, goals, and policies of the district.

8. Provide data to the board so it can make data-driven decisions.

9. Communicate with board members promptly and effectively.

10. Distribute information fully and equally to all board members.

11. Never bring a matter to a public meeting that is a surprise to the board.

12. Provide requests for additional information through a board update, special report, board agenda item, or as a board workshop or special meeting.

13. Represent the school district by being visible in the community.

14. Model the value of lifelong learning.

15. Be the instructional leaders of the district.

SOURCE: From Townsend (2005), *Effective School Board Meetings*. Thousand Oaks, CA: Corwin Press. Used with permission.

Resource B

Planned Priorities

XYZ Unified School District

Office of the Superintendent

SUPERINTENDENT OF SCHOOLS

Planned Priorities

Week of _____

- Cabinet/Agenda Setting

- All Administrators' Meeting

- Girls Math and Science Conference

- Board of Education

- Listening Visits

- Community/Public Relations

Date	Time	Subject	Place
Monday	9:00 a.m.	Cabinet	Room 228
	12:00 noon	Agenda Setting	Room 228
	1:00 p.m.	Teaching and Learning	Room 228
	3:00 p.m.	All Administrators' Meeting	Multi-Purpose Room
	5:30 p.m.	Three Staff Members	Superintendent's Home
Tuesday	7:30 a.m.	Leadership and Learning, Middle/High School Principals	Conference Room
	9:30 a.m.	Parents	Superintendent's Office
	11:30 a.m.	Listening Visit	Elementary School
	2:00 p.m.	Parents	Superintendent's Office
	3:00 p.m.	Phone Call	Superintendent's Office
	4:00 p.m.	Student Board Representatives	High School
	5:00 p.m.	High School Principals	Superintendent's Office
Wednesday	9:00 a.m.	Girls Math and Science Conference (bring greetings)	University
	11:45 a.m.	WASC Visitation Committee Meeting	High School
	1:00 p.m.	Board Member	Superintendent's Office
	2:00 p.m.	Board Member	Superintendent's Office
	3:30 p.m.	Classroom Conversations Taping	Elementary School
	5:45 p.m.	Board of Education-Closed Session	Middle School
	6:30 p.m.	Board of Education-Public Session	Middle School
Thursday	9:00 a.m.	Campus Tour	Leadership Public School
	10:50 a.m.	Listening Visit	Middle School
	1:30 p.m.	Parent	Superintendent's Office
	3:00 p.m.	Ad Hoc Committee (Site Acquisition)	Cabinet Room
	5:30 p.m.	HPSG Meeting	Chamber Office
Friday	9:00 a.m.	Meet for chartered bus	Facilities Operations Center
	10:30 a.m.	Campus Tour-High School	Out of Town
	12:00 noon	Rotary	In Town

Resource C

Civility Policy

CIVILITY POLICY

Members of the XYZ Unified School District staff will treat parents and other members of the public with respect and expect the same in return. The district is committed to maintaining orderly educational and administrative processes in keeping schools and administrative offices free from disruptions and preventing unauthorized persons from entering school/district grounds.

This policy promotes mutual respect, civility, and orderly conduct among district employees, parents, and the public. This policy is not intended to deprive any person of his or her right to freedom of expression, but only to maintain, to the extent possible and reasonable, a safe, harassment-free workplace for our students and staff. In the interest of presenting district employees as positive role models to the children of this district, as well as the community, the XYZ Unified School District encourages positive communication and discourages volatile, hostile, or aggressive actions. The district seeks public cooperation with this endeavor.

Disruptions

Any individual who disrupts or threatens to disrupt school/office operations, threatens the health and safety of students or staff, willfully causes property damage, uses loud and/or offensive language that could provoke a violent reaction, or who has otherwise established a continued pattern of unauthorized entry on school district property, will be directed to leave school or school district property promptly by the superintendent, principal, or designee.

If any member of the public uses obscenities or speaks in a demanding, loud, insulting, and/or demeaning manner, the administrator or employee to whom the marks are directed will calmly and politely admonish the speaker to communicate civilly. If the abusing party does not take corrective action, the district employee will verbally notify the abusing party that his or her participation in the meeting, conference, or telephone conversation is terminated, and, if the meeting or conference is on district premises, the offending person will be directed to leave promptly.

When an individual is directed to leave under the above circumstances, the superintendent, principal, or designee shall inform the person that he or she will be guilty of a misdemeanor in accordance with, for example, California Education Code 44811 and Penal Codes 415.5 and 626.7 if he or she reenters any district facility within 30 days after being directed to leave, or within 7 days if the person is a parent/guardian of a student attending that school. If an individual refuses to leave upon request or returns before the applicable period of time, the superintendent, principal, or designee may notify law enforcement officials.

Safety and Security

The superintendent or designee will ensure that a safety and/or crisis intervention techniques program is provided to raise awareness on how to deal with these situations if and when they occur.

When violence is directed against an employee, or theft against property, employees shall promptly report the occurrence to their principal or supervisor and complete an Incident Report.

An employee whose person or property is injured or damaged by willful misconduct of a student may ask the district to pursue legal action against the student or the student's parent/guardian.

Documentation

When it is determined by staff that a member of the public is in the process of violating the provisions of this policy, an effort should be made by staff to provide a written copy of this policy, including applicable code provisions, at the time of occurrence.

In addition, in the wake of any violation of the provisions of this policy, the employee will immediately notify his or her supervisor and provide a report of the incident on a form, such as the one that follows.

INCIDENT REPORT

Name _____

Site _____ Today's Date _____

Date and Time (Approximate) of Incident _____

Location of Incident (Office,   _____   _____
Classroom, Hallway, etc.)

Name of Person You Are Reporting   _____   _____
(If Known)

Is this a parent/guardian or relative of _____ Yes   _____ No
a student at XYZUSD?

Did you feel your well being/safety   _____ Yes   _____ No
was threatened?

Were there any witnesses to   _____ Yes   _____ No
this incident?

Name(s) of Witness(es)   _____   _____

Were the police contacted?   _____ Yes   _____ No

Below, please describe what happened:

_____

_____

_____

_____

_____

If you need additional space, please use the back of this sheet. Thank you.

_____
Signature of Person Completing Form

A copy of this Incident Report should be sent to the appropriate supervisor.

Resource D

Mission Statement and District Goals

MISSION STATEMENT

The mission of the XYZ School District is to create for our students a dynamic learning environment that is safe, healthy, and based on mutual respect, cooperation, and support among students, staff, parents, and the broader community. Staff and parents serve as educators and positive role models for all students by helping them develop a sense of responsibility, character, creativity, and the skills to become successful, productive citizens of our democracy.

DISTRICT GOALS

- XYZ schools will develop an environment that is physically and emotionally safe and that promotes positive character traits.
- XYZ schools will have parents and community actively participate in positive school and learning experiences.
- XYZ schools will help all students experience measurable success in any program.
- XYZ schools will increase the number of students eligible for college and other powerful postsecondary options.
- XYZ schools will increase the quality of interaction between teachers and students.
- XYZ students will learn, in their schools, to live and work in a culturally diverse society where staff is representative of the cultures in the community.

Resource E

Strategic Plan

```
        MISSION STATEMENT

   Our mission is to develop a community
  of life-long learners, creative thinkers, and
        responsible individuals, by providing
      innovative, quality educational programs
        in a safe, supportive environment.
```

BELIEFS

We believe
- that children are our highest priority.
- that each person has an inherent dignity and unique worth.
- that each person has talent and potential.
- that knowledge is power.
- that learning is a lifelong process.
- that, together, our similarities and differences create a vital community.
- that education is the shared responsibility of the community.
- in the fundamental values of honesty, respect, and responsibility.
- in the pursuit of excellence.

PARAMETERS

- We will provide an inclusive environment where each student feels connected to his or her school.

- We will continue to offer a rigorous and challenging curriculum while providing opportunities for students to develop their unique interests.
- We will provide recruitment, staff development, and evaluation that result in the highest-quality staff for our students.
- We will provide an academic support system to ensure that every student has the opportunity to succeed.
- We will identify and actively address the needs of our diverse students, staff, parents, and community.
- We will commit our resources on a priority basis to items identified in the district's strategic plan.

STRATEGIES

Curriculum

We will provide and support a challenging, diverse curriculum that is accessible and connects students to the community.

Citizenship

We will model, mentor, and acknowledge programs and processes that foster compassionate, ethical, and responsible behavior.

Technology

We will implement a guided master plan to incorporate the use of technology in all aspects of instruction.

Communication

We will implement an interactive, communitywide communication network.

Staff Development

We will create and implement an innovative, comprehensive recruitment and staff development plan, producing a world-class workforce.

Student Connection

We will create programs and processes to connect each student to school, education, and community, and to foster personal well-being.

STRATEGIC PLAN PRIORITIES

Academic Year _____ to _____

1. Curriculum	4. Student Connection
Strategy	**Strategy**
We will provide and support a challenging, diverse curriculum that is accessible and connects students to the community.	We will create programs and processes to connect each student to school, education, and community, and to foster personal well-being.
Priorities	**Priorities**

• Address academic consistency
• Provide career/technical options
• Develop strategies to address the achievement gap
• Support expanded access
• Offer academic support
	• Analyze Healthy Kids Survey and publish findings
	• Create proactive response
	  o classroom strategies for student connection
	  o development and implementation of meaningful curriculum
	• Foster parent/community awareness and responsibility

2. Staff Development	**5. Citizenship**
Strategy	**Strategy**
We will create and implement an innovative, comprehensive recruitment and staff development plan, producing a world-class workforce.	We will model, mentor, and acknowledge programs and processes that foster compassionate, ethical, and responsible behavior.
Priorities	**Priorities**
• Create a site-driven staff development plan • Base staff development on strategic plan and WASC (Western Association of Schools and Colleges) goals	• Develop clear and consistent expectations for parents/students/staff • Provide cross-district collaboration opportunities for

	students, staff, parents, and community to discuss: ○ substance abuse ○ ethical behavior ○ relational aggression ○ parental responsibility • Implement the district committee's recommendation for the "Fresh Start" substance abuse program
3. Technology	**6. Communication**
Strategy We will implement a guided master plan to incorporate the use of technology in all aspects of instruction. **Priorities** • Implement a new student data system • Analyze the Total Cost of Operations (TCO) • Offer additional student opportunities • Provide teacher and classified technical support	**Strategy** We will implement an interactive, communitywide communication network. **Priorities** • Create and publish consistent expectations for parents, students, and staff • Maximize current resources for communication

Resource F

Superintendent's Evaluation Process

PURPOSE

- ✓ Assess the quality of the superintendent's work

- ✓ Take stock of the quality of the board and superintendent teamwork

- ✓ Ensure the superintendent is clear about the board's direction

- ✓ Recognize and give credit to the superintendent

- ✓ Target areas of focus for the coming year(s)

- ✓ Plan for corrective action if necessary

- ✓ Model the evaluation process for the district

- ✓ Understand the evaluation process firsthand

- ✓ Fulfill your contractual obligation to your employee

BASIC AGREEMENTS FOR THE MEETING

- ✓ Commitment to frank and honest communication

- ✓ Confidentiality

- ✓ Trust, openness

- ✓ Willingness to be introspective about the board members' role in creating and sustaining a team

FACILITATOR'S ROLE AND TASKS

✓ Facilitate the discussion and keep it moving

✓ Take notes of board comments on aspects of the evaluation

✓ Write a summary of the discussion in the form of a final evaluation

✓ Send the summary to each board member and superintendent

✓ If only minor changes, will rewrite the evaluation and send to superintendent for his or her and the board members' signatures

✓ If substantial changes, will confer with superintendent and the board president for the next step (This is unlikely to occur because we will work for consensus during the meeting)

✓ Based on the summary evaluation, draft the annual letter of recommendation for superintendent's file to be signed by the board president

Resource G

School District Budget Development Calendar

SCHOOL DISTRICT BUDGET DEVELOPMENT CALENDAR

November	**Board Meeting** Approve budget guidelines	Superintendent
December	Approve first interim report	Assistant Superintendent, Business
January	Governor economic address Potential mid-year cuts Next year process begins	Assistant Superintendent, Business
February	Staff reduction recommendations if necessary Board budget study session	Superintendent, Assistant Superintendent, Business
March	**Board Meeting** Notification of non-returning teachers	Superintendent, Assistant Superintendent, Human Resources
April	**Board Meeting** Draft of budget assumptions	Assistant Superintendent, Business
May	Current year closing process begins **Board Meeting** Final draft budget assumptions and preliminary budget information	Senior Accountant, Superintendent, Assistant Superintendent, Business
June	**Board Meeting** New budget approved	Superintendent, Assistant Superintendent, Business
September	**Board Meeting** Prior year unaudited actuals approved	Superintendent, Senior Accountant

Resource H

Budget Guidelines for Boards and Staff

1. Specific time lines will be established for board action.

2. The district will continue to provide an effective educational program that meets federal, state, and district mandates at all grades.

3. Enhancements will be based on the greatest impact on teaching and learning.

4. Augmentation input will be gathered from parents, faculty, staff, and board.

5. Collective bargaining commitments will be honored.

6. Salary and benefit levels will continue to attract and retain qualified people.

7. Equipment replacement will be funded in relation to available resources.

8. Increases/decreases in costs of services will be provided for (i.e., gasoline, electricity, insurance, trash, debt repayment, etc.).

9. Categorical programs shall be self-supporting, and where allowable, include allocations for indirect costs. Special education is recognized as not self-supporting but efforts will be made to this end.

10. A new goal, project, or program will specify required resources.

11. Department budgets will provide prior year actual expenditures and past years expenditures along with the proposed budget.

12. Projections will include associated salary and fringe benefit costs within each program area, recognizing required step, column, and longevity increases for all staff.

13. All funds maintained by the district in addition to the general fund shall be included in the budget document.

14. New one-time income shall be identified and appropriated only to support expenditures that are not ongoing costs.

15. Budgeted expenditures shall not exceed income.

16. Capital improvements and preventative maintenance shall be planned to preserve the use and value of existing facilities and equipment.

17. Potential expenditures will be identified as funds become available.

18. Education Foundation, PTA, and other contributors will be encouraged to make three-year commitments.

Resource I

School District Responsibility Chart

Assignment	Contact Person
Absence Forms	
Accident Reports	
Accounts Payable	
Accounts Receivable	
Afterschool Program	
Agency Liaison for Student Support	
Assessment of Students • Elementary Level • Middle School Level • High School Exit Examination	
Beginning Teacher Support and Assessment	
Benefits	
Block Grants	
Board Meetings and Agendas	
Board Policies	
Budget Development	
Business Partnerships	
Certificated Personnel	
Child Welfare and Attendance	

Assignment	Contact Person
Classified Personnel	
Contracts • Employee • Business • Nonpublic School/ Nonpublic Agency • Consultant Contracts • Construction	
Counseling	
Credentialing—Teachers and Substitutes	
Cumulative Records for Students	
Curriculum Development	
Custodial Services	
Data Disaggregation	
Emergency Preparedness	
Evaluation of Personnel— All Departments	
Expulsion Procedures	
Facilities	
Food Services • Receivables/Payables • Free and Reduced Lunch Program	
Gifted Students	
Gifts/Donations	
Grade-Level Meetings	
Graduation Requirements and Guidelines	
Grantwriting	
Health Services/Screenings	
Home Hospital Support	
Independent Study	

(Continued)

Assignment	Contact Person
Injury and Illness Prevention Program	
Instructional Time/Staff Development Reform	
Kindergarten Registration/ Screening	
Leaves	
Liability Insurance	
Library Services	
Mail Delivery to School Sites/ Interdistrict	
Maintenance and Operations	
Education Foundation	
Music Program Support	
Office of Civil Rights (OCR) Reporting	
Payroll—Certificated and Classified	
Personnel Directory	
Personnel—Hiring Approval	
Preschool Programs	
Press Releases	
Public Records Act—Time Lines	
Psychological Services	
Purchase Orders/Requisitions	
Recognition of Employees/ Service Awards	
Reimbursement Procedures	
Report Cards	
Residency Verification	
Resignations	
Risk Management	
Safety Committee—Districtwide	

Assignment	Contact Person
School Plans	
School Resource Officer Program	

Section 504
  • Students
  • Employees	

Substitute Recruitment	
Substitute Calling for All Sites	
Summer School	
Suspensions	
Teachers—New Selection and Orientation	
Technology—Administration, Instructional, Infrastructure/ Database/ Budget/ Textbook Adoptions	
Telephone System	
Textbook Ordering and Inventory	
Transportation • Transportation— Special Education	
Truancy	
Uniform Complaint Procedures	
Volunteers—Processing	
Warehouse	
Web/Web Sites	
Worker's Compensation	

References

Adams, S. (1996). *Dogbert's top-secret management handbook.* New York: HarperCollins.

Adrain, L. A. (1997). *The most important thing I know.* New York: MJF Books/Fine Communications.

Barry, D. (2004). *Wisdom from a young CEO.* Philadelphia, PA: Running Press.

Carter, S. L. (1997). *Integrity.* New York: Harper Perrenial.

Carter, S. L. (1998). *Civility.* New York: Harper Perrenial.

Cloke, K., & Goldsmith, J. (2000). *Resolving conflicts at work.* San Francisco: Jossey-Bass.

Drucker, P. L. (1993). *The effective executive.* New York: HarperCollins.

Eadie, D. (2005). *Five habits of high impact school boards.* Lanham, MD: Rowman & Littlefield.

Eadie, D., & Houston, P. D. (2003, February). Ingredients for a board-savvy relationship. *The School Administrator, 60*(2), 56–57. Retrieved May 15, 2006, from http://www.aasa.org/publications.

Frank, M. O. (1986). *How to get your point across in 30 seconds or less.* New York: Simon & Schuster.

Fusarelli, L. D., & Jackson, B. J. (2004, September). How do we find and retain superintendents? *The School Administrator, 61*(8), 56. Retrieved May 15, 2006, from http://www.aasa.org/publications.

Gladwell, M. (2000). *The tipping point.* New York: Back Bay Books/Little, Brown.

Goleman, D. L., Boyatzis, R., & McKee, A. (2002). *Primal leadership.* Boston: Harvard University Press.

Harvey, E., & Lucia, A. (1998). *Walking the talk together.* Dallas, TX: Performance System Corporation.

Johnston, G., Gross, G., Townsend, R., Lynch, P., Novotney, P., Roberts, B. et al. (2002). *Eight at the top: A view inside public education.* Lanham, MD: Rowman & Littlefield.

Kimball, D. (2005, January). The cornerstone relationship between CEO and board president. *The School Administrator, 62*(1), 6. Retrieved May 15, 2006, from http://www.aasa.org/publications.

Kouzes, J. M., & Posner, B. Z. (1997). *The leadership challenge.* San Francisco: Jossey-Bass.

Lencioni, P. (2002). *The five dysfunctions of a team.* San Francisco: Jossey-Bass.

Lyles, D. (2000). *Winning ways.* New York: G. P. Putnam.

Phillips, D. (1992). *Lincoln on leadership.* New York: Warner Books.

Ramsey, K. (2000, March). The interim superintendency. *The School Administrator, 57*(3), 26–32. Retrieved May 15, 2006, from http://www.aasa.org/publications.

Safire, W., & Safir, L. (1992). *Good advice.* Avenel, NJ: Wings Books.

Sample, S. (2003). *The contrarian's guide to leadership.* San Francisco: Jossey-Bass.

Senge, P. M. (1990). *The fifth discipline: The art & practice of the learning organization.* New York: Currency Doubleday.

Spillane, R., & Regnier, P. (1998). *The superintendent of the future: Strategy and action for achieving academic excellence.* Gaithersburg, MD: Aspen Publications.

Strauss, D. (2002). *How to make collaboration work.* San Francisco: Berrett-Koehler.

Townsend, R., Brown, J., & Buster, W. (2005). *A practical guide to effective school board meetings.* Thousand Oaks, CA: Corwin Press.

Zadra, D. (1999). *I believe in you: To your heart, your dream, and the difference you make.* Lynnwood, WA: Compendium.

Index

27/2
Gift

CORWIN PRESS

The Corwin Press logo—a raven striding across an open book—represents the union of courage and learning. Corwin Press is committed to improving education for all learners by publishing books and other professional development resources for those serving the field of PreK–12 education. By providing practical, hands-on materials, Corwin Press continues to carry out the promise of its motto: **"Helping Educators Do Their Work Better."**